'Gaw finds wonder in the dark￼￼ for me was his getting los￼ lute pitch black. Deep prim￼ ￼ake for gripping reading . . . Th￼ ￼ful and valiant plea for us all to see that, unlike in science fiction, light isn't always good.'

BBC Countryfile Magazine

'Matt Gaw shows once again that he is one of the most inspiring of our young nature writers, with a highly original journey into darkness and night.'

Stephen Moss, naturalist and author of The Robin: A Biography

'Enchanting, fascinating and written with real soul and sensitivity. Under the Stars lifts the mind and the imagination.'

Rob Cowen, author of Common Ground

'Lyrical, warm, and suffused with the magic of the night, Under the Stars does what all the best books do – it changes the way we look at our world.'

Patrick Barkham, author of The Butterfly Isles

Under the Stars

Under the Stars

A Journey into Light

Matt Gaw

Elliott&Thompson

First published 2020 by
Elliott and Thompson Limited
2 John Street, London WC1N 2ES
www.eandtbooks.com

This paperback edition first published in 2021

ISBN: 978-1-78396-582-3

9 8 7 6 5 4 3 2 1

A catalogue record for this book is available from the British Library.

Typesetting by Marie Doherty
Printed in the UK by CPI Group (UK) Ltd, Croydon, CR0 4YY

For Kathryn, the brightest star,
and anyone who wanders or works in the night.

Contents

Introduction

The snow clouds mean there is no visible sunset tonight. The sky does not burn and bruise; the hot yolk of the sun does not split and run across the horizon in gold, yellow and peach. The cold, white sky does not even blush.

Instead, the light thickens and clots as darkness begins to form. It seeps and smokes from between stands of pines planted an arm's-length apart. It rises from the shadows of my footsteps on the track, and wells up from the deep, frozen ruts made by 4×4s and forestry machinery that trundle through this plantation.

For more than an hour now I have tramped through the forest that grows a few miles from my home, its familiar ruler-straight rides sparkling with fresh spring snow that still falls in fat, bumblebee flakes. The trees drooping, smoored and smothered.

Now the world is about to transform again. Night is coming. Darkness will soon cover the forest as surely as any snow.

I can't remember the last time I was out at night. Not just out, camping, running or toddling home from pubs, but *really* out; walking and watching as the light fades, experiencing darkness creeping up with each passing minute, from mountain to meadow.

It was my ten-year-old son who had inspired this impromptu outing. The other day, as he argued for a later bedtime, he told me solemnly that the average human will spend twenty-six years of life asleep. Although he was still ushered complaining to his room, his words wormed their way into my brain. They made me realise that my experience of night was one of eyes moving sightlessly against lowered lids rather than a view of the changing shades of the nocturnal hours. Although he might not have meant it as such, it was also a rebuke; a reminder that for all of my life's apparent fullness, it was in fact being only half lived. And so, here I am. Venturing into the darkness.

Even though I've been waiting for it, almost willing the night to arrive, the physicality of twilight surprises me. Catches me off guard. The air itself is a tangible mesh. A veil or a threshold to be crossed; from daylight to nightlight. The shifts might be gradual, but they are also dizzying. The light fuzzes like the picture on an old TV set. All feels hazy, flickering and granular.

At first I trip with every other step, until my eyes begin to adjust to the lowering light. My hearing seems sharper too; more eager to pick up any rustle or snow-muffled fidget.

Slowly, slowly, the definition of day blurs. I can no longer see the falling snow, although I can feel it on my face. The trees web together, the colours and contrasts grey into graphite. A detailed landscape rewinds to a simple but exquisite pencil sketch. The horizon becomes smudged as earth fuses with heavens.

By the time I reach the northern edge of the forest it is gone 11 p.m. and it's as dark as it's going to get. With the moon new and the cloud smoking-room thick, the only source of light seems to be the snow itself; the smashed-glass sparkle of twilight replaced by a watery luminescence that creates a topsy-turvy world where the land is brighter than the sky. Only under the trees, where the snow did not reach, has light been fully lost.

Out of the forest, the sky is a thick cobweb-grey that clings to heath and field, bunching in lighter, wet swags around wind-sharpened drifts of snow and darkening around ink-blot patches of gorse and bramble. Fallow deer, disturbed by the sound of my slow, snow-crumping footsteps, break into a fat-bottomed, see-sawing run. Others follow, the call to movement simply imposs-ible to resist, until the whole herd pours over the path in front of me. They move as one, a liquid form that jumps, jinks and springs away from open land towards the trees to my right. I watch as they go, their black shapes lit by snowlight and their own flashing scuts. Every muffled hoof-strike reverberating deep in my chest.

I've seen deer on the move before, plenty of times, but during the day. There's something about the night-time world that made the experience feel more intense, my world reduced by darkness to a much more intimate one that we briefly inhabited together.

I've never really considered exploring the nightscape before. To me night has always been a dark and gloomy place. A solid, black bookend to day that inspires fear and anxiety. But here among the trees, cloud and snowglow, I can already see that night is not just one long stretch of unforgiving darkness, any more than daytime is constant bright blue sky. Night is full of its own subtle shades of light, capable of illuminating the landscape and inspiring in us a sense of connection and wonder. I feel a tingle of delight at the realisation that almost by accident I've ghosted into a different world.

I wake late to the shouts of my children outside in the snow, enjoying their gift from the night. My legs feel stiff, and the balls of my feet sore from the walk. A cup of tea, lukewarm, sits on the bedside table. The curtains have been opened and the sky is heavy. More snow is on the way. The cat pushes through the half-closed door and jumps onto the bed. A night-seeker and snow-hater. He rubs his cheeks hard against my duvet-swaddled ankles and curls into a purring ball. Paws lifted, chin raised. I fuss him and think about the woods. The snow. The deer. The shades of the night.

Certainly, the way the night was lit up has stayed with me. I wonder how it would have appeared without the clouds; how the soft slide from day to night would have been different; how starlight, glinting hard off snow, would have expanded the night beyond a tree-lined horizon. But the clouds were also part of the magic, obstructing the glow from towns: the streetlights of Bury St Edmunds to the south and of Thetford to the north.

On our relatively small but densely populated island, there are up to 9 million streetlamps (one for every eight people). Their glare, when combined with that of 27 million homes, offices, warehouses and factories, is scattered by atmospheric particles to create a sickly orange sky-glow capable of blotting out the nocturnal interplay of natural light – the ever-present glare of electricity chases away darkness and snuffs out the stars.

That is surely one of the reasons I, like so many others, have been guilty of ignoring the night. It's something that many of us rarely experience at length. For aeons humans have tried to push the night away. As the sun lowers we go inside, lock our doors and draw our curtains. We turn on our lights. Fire, the putrid luminescence of rotting fish, the burning bodies of oily seabirds, fireflies gummed to toes, yellow, fatty candles, gas lights and then electricity – all have been used to conquer and vanquish the hours of darkness, transforming them into a duller kind of day.

But after finally getting a glimpse of natural darkness, I want to explore more. I want to immerse myself in all the different types of light and dark that night has to offer: to feel moonlight on my skin, to see a hard frost of stars across a dark sky, and to understand what effect the ever increasing blaze of artificial light has on our natural rhythms, and those of other species. And I want to experience again how the changing, thickening light has the power to transform our world.

1

Bathed in Moonlight

I stand on the beach with my back to the sea, listening to the flat, rattling intake of breath as the water sucks away shingle. The sun is two-thirds hidden but still not quite set. It forms a thick, burning wedge still clearly visible above the soft, sandy bluff. It is a halo of light below the blush of the lower sky, a giant, blood-red flower that blossoms on the inside of my eyelids every time I blink.

The sky itself looks as though it is splitting, like an oil stored too long. The heavy sediments of the dark settle, while overhead the colours shift and merge like newly applied watercolours running into each other – reds and pinks, yellows and white. Only in the highest reaches of the atmosphere, where the sun's rays still shine from beyond the earth's curve, does the sky remain

1

a brittle, icy blue. I watch as a plane flies almost directly up, its vapour trail a thread of gold that sews the colours together; jetting from the new darkness to the old light of day.

I check my watch and turn around. It's nearly time.

I've always loved coming here to the coast of Covehithe, both for its quiet and for its unerring strangeness. Nestled between the genteel promenades of Southwold to the south and the fallen splendour of Lowestoft to the north, it is a place where the mild flatness of East Anglia slowly unravels into the sea; one of the first places in the country to see the sun and one of the first to lose it. At certain times of the month, the same is true of the moon. It's why I have come here this evening, to experience our most familiar light at night. A glowing changeling, whose light has directed travellers and bewitched all living things – man and moth alike.

I've been wondering if the moon still has that power. In a world of artificial lighting and technology most of us no longer need it for navigation. The generations-old understanding of its cycle, how the waxing and waning light signified both the passing of days and the changing of seasons, is being forgotten. The moon is melting into the background, into insignificance.

The sea continues to suck and lick. A tern calls, sharp and bidding. Over the horizon of the North Sea comes the moon. First a glow. Then a pale, pinkish cuticle that swells into a weakling light. It continues to rise, an ever-expanding, ever-brightening island until after only a couple of minutes she tears away from the membrane of water, dripping light onto the earth, shining back at the sunken sun. The birth of the full moon.

She hangs, impossible, a great, cratered kite. Her own seas, the large basaltic plains formed by volcanic activity but once mistaken for water, are all visible, dark against the light-coloured highlands. There, the eyes of the Sea of Showers and the Sea of Serenity, there, the nose of Seething Bay and there, the open-mouthed surprise of the Sea of Clouds and the Sea of Knowledge. The whole face of the moon is pinched pink, a result of particles in the atmosphere scattering the light, but it looks as if she is blushing with the effort of her steep climb. She is, as D. H. Lawrence said, 'Flushed, grand and naked, as from the chamber'.

I can't help but be struck by the size of her. Looming and luminous. Although an average distance of 384,400 km away, she seems much, much closer – as if she could be hit and toppled with a well-aimed stone. It is a trick of the eye, an illusion that makes the moon seem larger as it sits just above the horizon, the cause of which is still debated.

It is, I realise, the first time I have ever seen the moon rise, have watched her gather her silvery skirts and jump. Perhaps her ascent has always been masked by houses, by hills and trees. But also, I suspect I haven't really looked. The moon, as large as it is, seems impossible to ignore, yet I have done just that. My experiences have been limited: a brief glance at a bony crescent while putting out the bins; a glimpse of a first quarter lurking in the car's rear-view mirror. Sometimes there have been daytime sightings too, pigeon-egg pale. A fragile, dark-eyed stop-out.

Over the last few weeks I've been making a conscious effort to pay closer attention, to reconnect with the moon, to appreciate the way it illuminates the night. As long as there has been life on earth, it has been bathed in its light.

Perhaps it is the cycle of the moon, recorded in chipped bone and chiselled rock, that first planted the concept of eternity in the human consciousness. The wan light illuminating a way beyond nothingness, and the hope of some kind of return. It has certainly inspired stories, legends and gods in almost every culture. The moon, we still tell our children, is where a man lives. For the Maya, it was a female goddess, a mother, a grandmother, a rabbit. For the Romans, the moon was Luna, the two-horned queen of the stars; for the Greeks, it was Selene driving a snow-white chariot across the skies. To the Nordic Sami she is Mano, Manno, Aske or Manna. The moon was whittled by the sun to thin bone only to regrow; was an orphan fetching water; an immortal lover; a cracked teal's egg. The list goes on, stories that not only explain the moon's movement but pin the moon's rhythms and her soft light into the fabric of life, across continents and ages.

And then, in 1969, humans planted a flag in her. The goddess was disrobed and punctured by a staff-wielding man.

I can't help but wonder if Apollo 11, despite all its achievements, is in some way behind our disconnection from the moon. Perhaps part of its myth and magic died under the dusty heels of conquering American moon boots. A leap for mankind that killed a leap of faith. After all, why watch and follow something that is known to be not a shining goddess but dead rock?

Growing up, I was fascinated by the moon landings. I read books, magazines, put up posters and wore NASA T-shirts emblazoned with the moon's face. I dragged my parents countless times to the Science Museum in London where I would stand by the scale model of the lunar module. A giant tinfoil-wrapped monument. But I wasn't really there for the moon but for the men who went there. My fascination was with the myth of the explorer: Neil Armstrong, Buzz Aldrin, Michael Collins.

Perhaps science replaced the mystical, spiritual connection that had sustained humans for generations. The imperfect moon was rendered banal and everyday by dust-sample scrapes and lifted rock lumps, transformed almost overnight from a source of wonder and worship to a sign of human power.

To the west the sun has finally sunk. The dark begins to rise, creeping up the tinny, Anderson-like shelters of a distant pig farm and spilling shadow from blocks of reed that surround Benacre Broad. The twilights arrive, roll into one another. First civil twilight, the blue hour, the lower atmosphere still bright and colour filled, then, when the geometric centre of the sun is 6 degrees below the horizon, nautical twilight. In the distance, the lights of Southwold, just visible behind the dark jut of scalloped, crumbling cliffs, click on and flicker orange. The town's lighthouse sends out a white, winked pulse. The first stars begin to needle their way through as astronomical twilight begins. Dusk, the threshold of true night, is within touching distance.

Along the darkened beach, I can see how the wrack line has been feathered by the tide, the curling claw of waves marked out in patches of bare sand. I begin walking again, picking up strands of bladderwrack, the pressed-flat coral shapes of hornwrack and fronds of pink seaweed resembling the exposed blood vessels of a lung.

Out to sea, the moon is higher now and has shrunk to a normal size. Its light, no longer scattered by the rosy lens of the atmosphere, is clear and milk bright. It spills over water, sand and shingle, bouncing hard off shell shards and pale stone.

Moonshine is made up mainly of sunlight reflecting from the moon's surface, its apparent brightness changing with the moon's orbit, from 0 per cent at new moon through to 100 per cent at full moon. Even at its brightest, though, it is still 200 times dimmer than the darkest day. The rest of the moon's light also comes from the sun but is twice reflected; bouncing from the earth and then the moon before reaching the backs of our eyes. It is this planetshine, earthshine, that creates the moon's ashen glow, illuminating parts that are not lit by the sun. During a waxing crescent, when the sliver of the bright sunlit moon is growing, earthshine exposes the moon's surface beyond the terminator line, the division between the light and dark hemispheres. The old moon is in the new moon's arms.

While we understand the moon's movements and light, the story of its origin is still, essentially, a hypothesis put forward by American astronomers William Hartmann and Donald Davis. They proposed that around

4.5 billion years ago, the earth was struck by a body the size of Mars. During the collision the mantle and the core of both planets merged into what would become the new earth, while residual mantle and bits of core spun off into the earth's orbit, eventually fusing to form the moon.

I like the idea we are made of the same stuff, that there is a duality between earth and moon, but there's a sadness too, a separation. A planet swarming with animated cells endlessly circled by a lifeless moon. A child dancing with its calcified twin, which reflects back earthlight and sunlight, and has the power to transform the night sky.

During the full moon, not only is its face brighter than at any other time, but its light lasts from sunset to sun-up. In an age when the skies were not bleached by electricity, its continuous glow, described in Cumberland and some other northern counties as 'throo leet', was reported to have roused people from their sleep. Even now, friends have told me they've woken in the middle of the night to a light shining so brightly through the window they expected to see an emergency vehicle, or maybe dawn, but it was the moon.

The phases of the moon would once have been familiar, even second nature, to our ancestors. While their night-time world was undoubtedly darker than ours and probably more dangerous, they knew for at least half the month the moon would cast more light than any rushlight or guttering tallow.

Even when access to artificial light increased in the Early Modern Age, the darkness of the night sky remained a serious consideration for travellers in both towns and rural regions. It was both a beacon and a protector, referred to in collections of old proverbs, words and phrases from across England as the 'parish lantern'. Although not everyone appreciated its guiding light. The moon robbed home-raiders, rogues and thieves of the disguise of darkness. For the criminally minded, the footpads, the alley rats, the blades, streetwalkers, rakes and rogues, the name of the moon was spat with venomous fury: 'The Tatler'.

On nights when the moon is partially obscured by cloud, its brightness is still enough to give outlines, to give form to people and places. The American essayist and night explorer Henry David Thoreau, who said that the 'kinds of moonlight are infinite', added that the 'traveller's whole employment is to calculate what cloud will obscure the moon and what she will triumph over . . . In the after-midnight hours the traveller's sole companion is the moon. All his thoughts are centred in her.'

Even the diarist Samuel Pepys, who never seemed especially keen on walking at night, did so under the light of the 'brave moonshine'. Although he did have three or four armed guards to accompany him.

Tonight, navigating in the moonlight is easy. Effortless. The squinting, peering and owlish bobs of the head, a technique I've been forced to adopt to see my way on other darker expeditions, are thankfully not needed here. The moon is, as it has been for generations, a lantern.

On a night like this I can appreciate her lighting the way. But most of the time, we simply no longer need her – or at least we think we don't. In our brightly lit modern world, she has lost some of her purpose. There is something poetic about it; as we lose touch with the moon, she is actually moving away from us. Each year she inches 3.78 cm further into space. In billions of years' time, her light will be invisible to us and the earth, abandoned, will spin slow and lifeless.

The North Sea, even on the brightest of days, is a murky mix of cold colours. Swirling brown. Sludge green. But now its midnight-blue waters are marked by a band of gold that stretches from the horizon to shore. It is as if the sea has been coated with bright dust sloughed from the moon's back as she pulled herself from the water.

As I walk back north, the light seems to follow me. Syrup soft, an enchanting shimmer, it stops when I do. Speeds with my footsteps. The light is a golden cord that binds the moon to my movement, pulls me to it. I can't help feeling, alone on this beach, that there is something magical about it. Moonlight is mystery, love and romance. It has a transformative power.

Covehithe is always atmospheric. The erosion that chews into cliffs, bites through path and road, means you are never sure what beach you will be visiting. At the southern stretch, where I am now, Easton Wood is slowly toppling onto the beach. By day the marooned trees, stripped of bark, salt-blasted and wind-polished, can seem skeletal and stark; white bones revealed by an earth that is losing its skin. But in the moonlight they appear softer, their wood pale and otherworldly.

I dabble my toes in the sea, causing the reflected light to ripple into black and slowly re-form. I think how the marine creatures out there will be responding to the moon, its light sparking spring after a long winter. Scientific studies have shown that the reproductive organs of some molluscs and fish shrink with the new moon, before swelling, ready for shell-rattling orgies, at the full moon. It is a time of movement, of sex, of egg-laying and hatching. Each year, during the full moon of November, the sea around the Great Barrier Reef is full of egg and sperm, which spews in great plumes from corals to form mats of pink, orange and yellow.

The moon is not the only factor, but it seems to be the most important. Water temperature and day length also appear to be environmental cues for sexual synchronicity, yet if the moon is obscured by clouds the corals will not spawn. The reproductive frenzy is paused until the next full moon.

Similarly, land creatures are drawn from the shadows by the full moon to hunt and mate. *New Scientist* reporter Jessica Hamzelou[1] explains how night monkeys, or owl monkeys, the only nocturnal primates of the New World, hoot and jabber at the full moon. They fall silent as the angle of the moon changes and the shadow of the terminator line creeps again.

I think of the last full moon, and how I walked to what has become one of my favourite places to haunt at night, a place near Lackford in Suffolk, where the River Lark runs dark in its small cut under the trees. The moon, casting a shivelight through willow and alder, had silvered leaves and turned the water to a dusty barn-owl white. Although I couldn't see the moon directly, I remember how the woods, the water, the very earth under my feet felt different. The whole place seemed to thrum with scuttling, clattering, chattering life. The foxes yipped and *wow-wow-wowed* with renewed vigour, muntjac hacked their raw smoker's cough, badgers ploughed noses through soil with wormy intent. Even the spiders seemed more industrious. Their silken snares seemed to cross every path and space between the trees, stretching and snapping over my face as I walked.

Human society seems to have been impacted by the changing stages of the moon's light as well. The waxing of the moon towards fullness, with its fleeting power to light up the darkness, has long been associated with sex and birth, with the planting of seeds. A full moon has different names, according to the seasons: the Wolf Moon of January, the Snow Moon of February, the Worm Moon of March, when the ground is soft enough for casts to once again be made in the thawed ground.

The moon hanging above the sea now is the first of spring. The Egg Moon, the Sprouting Grass Moon, the Pink Moon, named not for the colour of her cheeks, but for the early flowers that once covered the plains of North America. It is a moon that signals new life, a promise of burgeoning warmth. The following wane is a time of diminishment. A sign to treat the sick, to bring in the crops. To prune and geld.

But perhaps the effect goes deeper, influencing our minds and souls. It has long been believed that her silvering light brings with it madness and mayhem. The word 'lunatic' is derived from the Latin word for moon: *luna*. The moon's influence over the tides, a gravitational pull that causes even rocks to bulge towards the moon, inspired the idea that the earth's satellite could also move moisture around the human body, changing 'humors' and twisting psyches. The belief, which continued through to the medieval period, was even revived by Newtonian physics. Richard Mead, a contemporary of Newton and physician to King George II, argued that conditions such as nephritis, ulcers, hysteria and epilepsy all followed the moon's cycle.

Even now, there are countless groups who swear by the moon's power. Some organic farmers follow a biodynamic pattern that is strongly influenced by the moon's cycle. My late grandad, a true man of the earth, trusted only the heavens when it came to his carrots, planting them religiously in the wax of the moon. For astrologers, the moon is linked to, or signifies, moods and emotions. For pagans, hedgewitches and druids, the moon is both an inspiration and intensely spiritual.

Countless others – a quick internet search will yield eye-opening results – are still convinced of the moon's significance when it comes to sexual pleasure. Earlier this very night, as the sun set, I saw a series of flashes, an electric pulse that formed dancing spots on my eyes and set off the terns, gulls and ringed plover that had already gone down to roost in the shingle and marram grass surrounding the Broad. Raising my binoculars, I had focused the lens, expecting to see a photographer capturing the sunset. Instead I saw a woman with a bright red skirt raised above her waist as she bent forward to touch her toes, wiggling her exposed bottom like a duck settling on water, while a man crouched down to take photographs. Another Pink Moon on Covehithe beach.

It would be easy to write off all the moon believers as eccentric, as kooky. As lunatics. But if the moon's light has such a clear effect on so many of earth's creatures, why should it not also have an impact on us?

The idea even holds among some of our most respected professions. Doctors, nurses, police officers and midwives have all gone on record in support of the lunar myth: the idea that our hospitals, birthing suites and custody cells become busy when the moon is full.

A recent study by researchers at the Université Laval in Québec City, Canada, revealed that 80 per cent of nurses and 64 per cent of doctors believed that they saw more people with mental-health problems during a full moon.[2]

However, studies have found no connection between the moon and human behaviour. The effects our emergency workers have observed could easily be explained away by confirmation bias. The full moon is simply ignored when the nights are quiet. Science tells us that the water in our brains does not conform to the tides. Menstruation, mental illness, sex and crime are born of flesh and circumstance, not from the moon's gravity.

Yet we are still drawn to the moon – to its myths and its mysteries. We are still convinced of its powers. Even at a time when the moon is so often ignored, we appear to cling to that sense that something bigger than ourselves is at work beneath illuminated skies.

I don't need to check my watch. I can see from the spray of stars that the last stage of twilight is long over. True night has arrived. It is now as dark as it will get in the open, where some form of light usually still touches the landscape. Only under the cover of trees or within the wet maw of caverns and caves, where starlight and moonshine never reach, will the surroundings be a true and fathomless black.

In a few moons, as summer arrives, the sun will never sink 18 degrees below the horizon. Technically twilight will stretch from sunset to dawn. While the effect might be subtle in the southern reaches of the UK, it is more pronounced in the north. At the poles, where the summer sun never sets, twilight is not measured in hours but weeks.

I keep walking north, past where I came on to the beach, heading away from the lights of Southwold towards Kessingland. With the moon high overhead, the only real darkness comes from me. My shadow, skittering over the stones, is thicker, stickier than during the day. With no airlight – light that comes from the sky as opposed to direct sunlight – moon shadows are pure, inky black. I watch mine out of the corner of my eye. It seems that if I were to make a sudden movement, it would lag behind, or dance away off the beach. It reminds me of Peter Pan chasing his runaway shadow.

On a sandy bluff out of reach of the tide I set up a bivvy and sleeping bag, and crawl inside. I don't intend to sleep, but I do, drifting in and out, the moon gliding across the sky with each hour-long blink.

Slowly, slowly, twilight arrives again, blue light returns to the upper atmosphere, forcing the darkness down. The moon is sinking, setting, its face already scratched by trees and hedgerows. Its light little more than a jellyfish glow.

I had always considered that the myths of the moon, its creation fables, the legends of its power, belonged to the past, to a landscape of imagination. But after my night of moonbeams, these stories make sense now. The moon hasn't lost her power to inspire us, to make us search for understanding beyond ourselves. Embracing night, drinking up moonlight, is part of our culture and our nature. Caught up in our baubles of man-made light, it's easy to take her familiar face for granted. But here at Covehithe, where the moon's reflected light is not dampened by the flare of electricity, her ethereal glow highlights a connection between all humans, all life, that is or was.

This year has been good for moon watchers. In January, the skies were lit by not one, but two full moons. The second, described as a blue moon, was also a super moon – 14 per cent larger than average and 30 per cent brighter – on its closest elliptical orbit to the earth. Typically, blue moons take place only every two or three years, but the phenomenon happened again in March.

And so, a month after my first trip, I return to Covehithe, hoping to see another lunar phenomenon: a lunar eclipse – the longest of the twenty-first century. A time when the most distant and smallest full moon of the year passes through the centre of the earth's shadow. For a few hours, the sun, earth and moon will line up, and the earth's shadow will block all direct sunlight reaching the moon. The only light reflected by the lunar surface will come from the sun's rays, refracted through the earth's atmosphere. As with sunset and sunrise, the blue light

21

will scatter and only the shorter-wavelength red light will get through. The moon will turn to rust or, as eclipse moons are also known, to blood.

For our ancestors such changes to the moon's light were seen as a sign of foreboding and birthed many myths rooted in fear. The full moon's magical light would be slowly and unexpectedly consumed, the bright night made darker and ominous. For the Incas, the blood moon was interpreted as the result of a jaguar attack. They feared that this light-eater, after gorging on the moon, would turn on the earth. They faced it as they would face a wild beast: brandishing weapons, urging their dogs to howl and snarl, hoping to drive it away.

Hindu folk tales link the lunar eclipse with the demi-god Rahu consuming the elixir of immortality. The sun and the moon attack him, slicing through his neck. But the cleaved head lives on and, in retaliation for his injuries, swallows the moon, which reappears, full but blood-soaked, from Rahu's severed gullet.

In the scriptures of Christianity, the reddening moon is a sign of God's wrath and a portent of Judgement

Day. Perhaps this is why, despite the abandonment of the lunar calendar, Easter still falls on the weekend after the spring full moon. Easter Sunday can never be lit by a blood moon. Even now the apocryphal properties of a lunar eclipse are still seized on by Christian fundamentalists. A couple of days ago, I think as a joke, a friend sent me a video of an online sermon delivered by evangelist Pastor Paul Begley about tonight's full moon. Dressed in a loose jacket and looking more like a car salesman than a prophet of doom, he cheerfully read from the Book of Joel, claiming the eclipse was a sign of the second coming of Christ. A time of salvation for believers, damnation for everyone else: 'The Sun shall be turned into darkness, And the Moon into blood, Before the coming of the great and awesome day of the Lord.'

At Covehithe, there are already people on the beach. One man sits alone, his back against a sandy bluff, shoes off, staring intently out to sea. There are mostly couples here, talking quietly, as if a raised voice might prevent the moon from raising its head. Tonight I have company too. My friend Shaun has come along, eager to experience the quiet of the night, the magic of the moon. But also, if this is to be the end of days, a reckoning of souls under the bloodlight of the moon, I don't want to be damned on my own.

The sun is setting but no one is looking west. Instead all eyes are focused on the east, scanning the horizon, looking for the moon to rise red out of the sea. Waiting for the rapture.

But after nearly two weeks of heat, which was as unseasonal as the spring snow, the weather is threatening to break. Storm clouds are beginning to gather. Folding and massing as though they are locking together into heaped grey piles, their white fringes darkening like wetted cloth. We stare at them, hoping for a hint of brightness, a clue to the moon's whereabouts.

At Southwold, five miles down the coast, the first sparks of lightning are forking down around the lighthouse. The sudden brightening of the landscape feels unsettling, so unlike the steady light of the moon when I was last here. The muscles of the eyes tense and relax with the throb of the clouds. Although we can hear no thunder, the horizon is smudged, a sure sign that rods of rain are falling to earth just a few miles away.

The wind and the lightning strikes are increasing in intensity. To the south, west and east they glare over the land and out to sea, illuminating plumes of dust being blown from fields to twist around the square tower of Covehithe's church. I think of Pastor Paul and his bad moon rising. Terns fly in from the sea, straining muscle and sinew against the wind, their laboured wing-strokes accompanied by *screech-scrack* calls like unoiled hinges. Even the waves are running for cover, pushed northwards, black and razor-backed.

The storm edges closer, surrounding us. It pincers and prods, shading in patches of light where the twilight is yet to reach. The sky should be dark, but not like this. The blackness, oily and thick, has been magnified by the heavy cloche of clouds. Yet the darkness never holds for long. Sheet-lightning flashes turn the clouds to papery, orange lanterns while forked bolts seem to split land and sea. Sometimes the lightning doesn't even seem to hit the earth but twists back up into the sky like a horse-shoe of fire, the white heat bending away from the cold of the North Sea. My eyes, now adjusted to the night, are seared by each lick of light. A burst directly in front of us forms three horizontal lines, a three-bar fire, that stripes my vision.

The whole beach, now empty save for Shaun and me, is storm-lit, the wavering, strobing flashes making me feel as if I'm standing in a Turner painting. The church is the Slave Ship, surrounded by lightning-burnt swirls of dust.

I can't help but wonder if standing on a flat beach as an electrical storm approaches is a good idea. There is a reason everyone has left. I think of being hit by a billion volts, a jolt that travels from tip to toe and turns sand to glass. I ask Shaun if he's worried. He looks at me, weighing it up.

He shouts over the wind, 'Nah. It will hit the biggest thing.' He grins. 'You're two inches taller than me.'

And then it arrives. The sound catches up with the light. A noise like a thousand dropped bowling balls, a gut-thumping, sonorous grumbling. The rain follows. Hard. Heavy. Cold as the sea, it drums and explodes on our heads and upturned faces.

We laugh as our T-shirts are pasted to our chests and our hair is gummed to our foreheads, opening our mouths wide so the rain might land on our tongues. Iron. Fresh. Sweet. The sharp coolness, after the warmth of day, is delicious. Deliriously so. We whoop and holler, standing with arms outstretched, like lunatics under the sheathed blood moon.

This is not what we had hoped for, but the night is full of mystery, surprises and wild forces we can't control, and of different kinds of light we can't anticipate. The disappointment of missing the eclipse, never seen, now over, is outweighed by the exhilaration and drama of the lightning strikes, which I still feel scribbled on the back of my retinas. I feel alive and excited at the prospect of discovering all the other secrets the night sky holds.

2

Under the Stars

The track winds through the woods and then begins to climb. Through deer gates, over cattle grids and a fenceless, narrow wooden bridge, the car wheels just inches above a burn that churns over rock and stone. A final hairpin, a tyre-spit of sand and grit, and then I can see it. The Scottish Dark Sky Observatory, its white dome a bauble of light against the spruce-thick pitch of the Galloway Forest that stretches for 373 square miles to the south.

I've come to Scotland with my family under the guise of a holiday. A getaway break to a country we all love. But, also, Scotland is where the night lives.

Above my desk at home I have pinned a map, formed from photographs taken by a weather satellite of Britain at night. It is a map of night's retreat. The island is a feverish rash of yellow, orange and hot pinks. Towns and cities stand out like colourful welts against the darker shades of the countryside and patches of coast. London is by far the brightest point of light, surrounded by the lurid varicose veins of roads that wind and knot to the heart of the country, to Birmingham, Nottingham and the major towns of Lancashire and Yorkshire.

Yet away from the band of lights that stretches across Scotland's slender throat, there are greater areas of darkness: on the Highlands, so cruelly cleared of people in the eighteenth and nineteenth centuries, across mountains, around coast and forest sprawl. All are coloured on the map by the darker pixels of charcoals and deep, bottomless blues.

I had to come here.

I park the car and walk to the edge of the hill, which faces north. Nestled in a bowl of hills I can see Dalmellington: a one-swing, one-shop rural town, whose road sign welcomes careful drivers 'to the town in the stars'.

Spending a night under the moon had given me a chance to experience how its light has the power to transform our surroundings – and us. I had felt part of the natural world in a way that I rarely have during the day. Furthermore, it gave me a new appreciation for the moon as a lantern, a realisation of how important its brightness is in a place that is free of artificial light. But it also left me wondering what it would have been like without that familiar beacon to navigate by. How it would feel to wander under a sky lit only by the stars.

I think stars are overlooked, perhaps even more than the moon. Partly it is because they are almost invisible to so many of us, smothered and outshone by the bright glow of urban sprawls. In the Early Modern Age the stars were brighter and more plentiful, important indicators of time, place and season. If the moon slumbers, wrote the poet Robert Herrick, 'The stars of the night will lend thee their light.' I've heard it said that in some dark-sky locations, where conditions are still similar to on those naturally dark nights of history, stars can even cast shadows.

I had a taste of the stars at Covehithe but now I want more. I want to see how their prickling light is different from the moon's soft, white wash. But I'm also fascinated by how they can make us feel. Stars, despite their beauty, have always scared me a little. I'm intimidated by their number. Confused by their names and changing positions. Overwhelmed by their distance from us, knowing that their glimmering light has taken millions, even billions, of years to reach us. Theirs is a scattered buckshot of light that I can make little sense of. Perhaps my discomfort comes from being forced to acknowledge the vast scale of our universe, and the tiny space we occupy in it. That's why I wanted to come here, to explore those thoughts, to experience a place where stars abound, where the night burns with an ancient light that will outlast us all.

After a day of spitting rain and wind that could never settle on a direction, the weather is calm and the clouds seem to be parting. A few sheep are calling and somewhere, perhaps in the steep valley I've just driven through, the first tawny owl is *ke-wick*-starting its nocturnal patrol.

I'm early – I'm always early, it is a pathological quirk that my wife Jen is working hard to iron out – but there are other people here already. At the door of the larch-lapped observatory a man wearing a Dark Skies lanyard identifying him as David Warrington, the observatory's resident astronomer, is being quizzed by three Americans. They want to go for a walk before the star-gazing session starts but are worried about wildlife. Not wildlife, but Wildlife. Bear. Lynx. Wolves. Things that come out at night with tooth and claw.

Inside, the observatory is surprisingly big. I walk around a museum that contains telescopes, panels explaining the history of space missions and moon land-ings, and a glass case that contains an iron meteorite the size of a small owl pellet. The note underneath explains it is thought to be 3 billion years old; a time when life on earth was just beginning to surge.

We've been told to gather in the observatory's main room, which has been set up with two crescents of chairs. A projector is casting images of stars, stitched together from decades of satellite photographs of deep space, onto the curved wall and ceiling. Stars and galaxies appear in bursts of gassy reds and hazy blues while the video's narrator competes with a loop of electronic astral music. A few more people drift in. Taking their seats quietly, unzipping coats and removing layers. The American tourists come in too, unscathed by megafauna or major incident, clutching bags of books and pens purchased from the observatory gift shop.

David appears, looks around the room, down at a clipboard of names and checks his watch. A dozen more people are yet to arrive but he's keen to get going. There's good reason. The skies here may be dark but the weather is unpredictable, with cloud, rain or snow blacking out the stars and limiting viewing to a rough average of one night in five.

It was November 2009 when the forest became the UK's first and the world's fifth international dark-sky park. There are now sixty-two, including sites at Bodmin Moor, Northumberland's Kielder Forest and the Elan Valley in Wales. They are places where the night is protected for its scientific, natural, educational and cultural value, where the stars still gather in large numbers and the Milky Way still smudges the sky. For many people the Scottish Dark Sky Observatory is a first taste of a really dark night – and of the light that emerges from it.

'Most people live in places where the glow of artificial light will trespass into their lives,' David explains. 'It's something that can impact on your health and on wildlife, but also it shines up into the sky, blocking the view of the stars.'

'For us, the observatory is about trying to raise awareness of light pollution, so in future everyone can start to have darker skies. It's about just having light where we need it and making sure that lights aim down rather than being allowed to escape elsewhere.'

He points north. Beyond the soft twinkle of Dalmellington, whose lights have in the past month been converted to modern, 'dark-friendly' lighting, is Scotland's central belt. The domes of light from Ayr, Kilmarnock and Glasgow are clear to see: glaring into and reflected back by the clouds. Acidic. Orange. An Iron Brew sky.

Tonight there is a new moon, meaning there is no competition for the stars, and above us they begin to appear as the night slowly thickens. We take it in turns to look through the telescope as David points out the things of interest. There are our planetary neighbours – Jupiter, with two of its seventy-nine moons, Ganymede and Calisto, glinting like grains of gold, the yellow marble of Saturn with a dust-bunny fuzz of a ring, the dull red of storm-lashed Mars – and even in the early stages of the night the brightest stars: Vega, Alpha Lycrae, Arcturus and Alpha Bootis, the most luminous star of the summer. Alpha Bootis is 8.5 billion years old, 36.6 light years away and 170 times more luminous than our sun. A red giant that has exhausted its core fuel of hydrogen and is now burning through its shell. Consuming itself.

We change telescopes, entering the main rooftop observatory, where a segment of the 5-metre dome has been opened to let in the night. As I look through the eyepiece, my eyelashes brushing the glass, David explains we are looking at a globular cluster in the constellation of Hercules. Less poetically, it is known as M13. I squint, trying to focus. Then something smokes from the blackness. A spider's egg sac of light, a zygote waiting to split. Hundreds on hundreds of stars yoked together. I half expect some to fall away, to scuttle. To form new kaleidoscopic shapes in front of my eyes. I wouldn't have argued if I'd been told I was looking through a microscope rather than a telescope.

The telescope is refocused again and again. Probing for bigger stars, smaller stars, cool stars with red glows, hot stars with icy-white heat. Our eyes stretch beyond our own galaxy of the Milky Way to the pale haze of Andromeda 2.537 million light years away. We stare, we gasp; drunk on starlight.

Telescopes like the ones at this observatory have for centuries helped humans reach further into the night sky. In 1609, Galileo Galilei turned the Dutch-invented spyglass upwards and saw that dark gulfs of the sky were in fact filled with stars. Bigger lenses were ground and telescopes grew rapidly in size. By 1670 the largest telescopes were no longer hand-held but measured as much as 15 metres. At the end of the seventeenth century they were three times that length, their giant tubes refracting more and more distant light.

The best modern telescopes can see stars a staggering billion times fainter than the eye can see. In a conversation with Paul Bogard in his book *The End of Night*, the

American astronomer Bob Berman compares it to being able to see a cigarette from 125,000 miles away.

In theory, the naked eye, while many times weaker than a telescope, is capable of seeing around 5,000 stars. However, half of these are hidden by the earth at any one time. More are lost by the extinction on the horizon (the scattering of light by air molecules and particulates) and light pollution extinguishes many more.

It's hard to avoid the irony. As we advance towards the stars with greater technology and an understanding that reaches far beyond what we can see, we are also in retreat from them. The trappings of modernity have helped to hide them in a sickly soup of man-made light.

Altair, or Alpha Aquilae, is one of the closest stars visible to the naked eye, just 16.7 light years away. But there is no 'just' about it. Aboard a space shuttle, which can travel 5 miles a second, it would take 621,240 years to reach. The science is as poetic as myth. The scales and figures are too large to comprehend. Stars that dwarf the sun, a star itself that is too massive for us to comprehend, whose age is double that of the earth. Distances many times longer than a human life. The very large, like the very small, is hard to grasp.

I drift away from the group and go back outside onto the observatory roof. The night has grown cold. Seeing so many stars in such detail has been amazing but it all feels like a lot to take in – and it hasn't done much to change how overwhelmed they make me feel. The experience of looking through the telescope reminds me of the Total Perspective Vortex in Douglas Adams' *Restaurant at the End of the Universe*: a machine built with the intention of showing beings the infinity of creation, that has become used as an instrument of torture. 'For when you are put into the Vortex you are given just one momentary glimpse of the entire unimaginable infinity of creation, and somewhere in it a tiny little marker, a microscopic dot on a microscopic dot, which says, "You are here."'

The realisation of the smallness, the insignificance of the self is certainly enough to shred the brain. But it does also give you a different perspective. A chance to step back from our individual worries and fears and see how small they really are in the vast and ancient reaches of space. To know that beyond our short, flaring lives, something bigger will endure.

I look up to a sky that bursts with natural light. The largest stars pebble bright; the palest clustering together to form a salt spray hardened onto the black sackcloth of night. Yet, the night is no single fabric. In the darkness of Galloway there are textures and depths I have never seen before. The sky, which I've long thought of as a smooth dome stretching from horizon to horizon, has been broken open to reveal stars that are distant and closer, bright and dim, hot and cool. It reminds me of looking at the seabed through clear waters, where rocks, trenches, sand bars and seaweed can also be seen – yet the perspective, the idea of depth, is almost impossible to grasp.

Earlier, David had shown us how to get a foothold in the night sky, using asterisms (the often-familiar shapes, like the Plough, not officially recognised by the International Astronomical Union) and the constellations. The names had tripped from his tongue as he pointed out the dot-to-dot patterns, unwinding their stories, their meaning: there, the asterism of the Summer Triangle, formed by Vega, Deneb and Altair, itself kissed by the swan neck of Cygnus; the long swoop of the Serpent; the Plough, the arse end of the Great Bear, whose saucepan points the way to the North Star, Polaris.

In all there are eighty-eight officially recognised constellations. The most familiar, the zodiac constellations (which are on the ecliptic, the path of the sun) come from the myths of Rome and Greece. From north to south, west to east, there are stars that are hunters. Stars that are the hunted. They are nymph and nomad, animals and god. Rogues killed or punished. They are stars whose rise and fall signal seasons and sea-going. They are sisters, they are daughters, mothers, brothers and fathers. They are ancestors.

The Milky Way is now clearly visible. Like the constellations, it is rooted in Greek myth. Galaxy is derived from *galaxias*: milk. The legend is that Zeus allowed his son Heracles, born of the mortal Alcmene, to suckle from his divine wife Hera. She awoke and pushed him away, the resulting spurt of milk forever staining the night sky.

It's a spectacular sight, a splash of hazy light made up of hundreds of billions of stars. Yet the glowing arm of the galaxy that contains our own solar system is no longer visible to 77 per cent of the UK population who are swathed in a luminous fog. Many adults and children, my own included, have never seen it. And so they do not mourn it. The baseline for what we expect at night, the starlight that we expect to see, has over time warped and fallen to new lows. The constellations have come unstrung, the shared cultural experience of generations, a sense of place and perspective, along with a light older than humans, gods, the earth, have all been lost.

I wish now I had brought the kids tonight to see the stars rather than tucking them into bed. Part of it was selfishness. I knew they would complain at the cold, would grow restless with the queues for the telescopes and grumble at the car ride. But surely this sight would have left them quietly star-struck.

The group is drifting off now, but I continue to gaze upwards at a sky streaked by light and dark; millions of stars that cannot be prised apart by the eye. I follow the black ink of the interstellar dust of the Great Rift that tears through the Milky Way's heart. The night cracked and dazzling.

The scale is simply impossible. The stars rush towards me, while also being utterly unreachable. I wonder if it's the earth's curve that creates the dizzying perspective or just the sheer size of it all. It is mind-bending. I feel a whirling vertigo as if I'm being lifted up. I hold onto the railing, trying to anchor myself. For a few seconds there is nothing but the night sky. No sound, no smell or taste. But it is not just a visual experience. It is physical, as if every nerve, every synapse, has lit up in reply to the stars.

The lighthouse is winking on Ailsa Craig as I set off. A lonely flash from the small island. Home to gannets and puffins and not much else. Behind it, across the froth-trimmed waves of the outer Firth of Clyde, the slumped shadow of Arran and the Mull of Kintyre. Darkest of mountains with valleys of green.

The last cinder of the sun is burning towards the water. High in the sky, the clouds are thick and heavy but the lower reaches are still clear. It looks like a child's drawing. A line for the sea, a gap, then a line for the sky. The night will reconnect them, fill in the space. Rushing over wave and rock to colour the air and eye with its velvet, salt-tanged shade.

It takes about an hour to reach the Wood of Cree. My friend Will had told me about this place. He used to work here, managing what is the largest fragment of native, temperate rainforest in the south of Scotland. He warned me that the 690 acres of wood and heath are easily big enough to get lost in. In fact, he laughed when I said I wouldn't have a torch, he thought I was joking. 'Oh, man, it'll be dark in the woods,' he said. 'Really dark.' But I don't plan to spend much time among the trees. It's the stars I've come to sit among.

In my head I've planned to leave the car somewhere and walk beyond the woods to a clearing where I'll be able to see the sky clearly and find my way back using only the stars to navigate. Last night, with the memory of the observatory only twenty-four hours old, I practised mapping the starlight. I found the Summer Triangle, the North Star, I even used my fist as a crude sextant, seeing if my rough reckonings matched the land. I feel confident. Perhaps too confident.

I gather my gear and set off, but decide to wait for the dark to rise by a pool flanked by plantation and hills. Above them the icy mare's tails of cirrus clouds are the colour of blood orange. The water, perfectly still, reflects it all. To the north, the pool almost touches the horizon and it is as if the sky has overflowed into this shallow basin. The lake is not spring-fed but sky-fed. Further away I can still see the thicker clouds gathering, sweeping in off the sea.

The temperature is already dropping. A light mist creeps in, the air cooling more quickly than the water's surface, and smooths away the blisters of rising fish, leaving just half the pool visible.

It is then the dog otter appears, porpoising playfully through lily pads and reed, his movements rumpling the water's surface like bed sheets. I watch with my binoculars as he dives, his tail plopping under the surface, whipping away rags of mist.

He surfaces again close to the opposite bank. He scrambles out; his rounded, tomcat head tousled and deliciously wet. He rolls, skitters and runs. An odd hump-backed gambol, his movements are almost non-stop.

He sniffs, spraints and then slides back into the pool. Melts into the mist and water, pours himself in like oil. Gone.

By the time I leave the pool the clouds have darkened the sky to an end-of-twilight pitch. Part of me regrets not wearing a watch, so I could check to see if night really has arrived, but that's really not the point. I'm worried that I could become overly reliant on these signals. I want to feel them, rather than 'know' them. Night has its own time, its own feeling, and while I'm here I want to abide by it.

Away from the water and the openness of the pool the world is darker still. The air itself dew-damp and sooty. There is little detail in the land, only definition: the black shapes of the wood, crouched on the hill, while above the treeline on the south horizon, Jupiter is bright. It strobes through heavy lids of scudding cloud that cover much of the sky. Blinking in and out. In and out.

I turn east and head up a trail that is identifiable as a navigable route only because it is slightly darker than its surroundings. The entrance of the wood drips with night's shade. It is not so much a space to walk into but a hole to be fallen into. I pause and take a deep breath. I feel nervous. Anxious. Afraid of getting lost, afraid of being afraid. A paragon of ridiculousness: a night walker nervous of the night. My earlier confidence already seems misplaced.

I feel my way through a kissing gate and begin to walk, the dark rushing in after just a couple of tentative steps. Viscous. Thick. Tangible. I repeatedly rub my eyes with the backs of my hands. It is a subconscious act, as if I might clear my eyes, wipe the dark away. Yet my hands are pretty much all I see. The skin flashing pale like fish beneath the surface of some Stygian flow.

There is little rhythm to my walking. It is a step, then a breath, then another step. A zombie stagger with arms outstretched, my body tense and alert. Humans react more quickly to sound than to sight, and at night, when sound waves bend towards the cool earth, that effect is amplified. I bate like a bird of prey at noises in the canopy: the crack of deer through scrub, the gunshot wing flap of a disturbed roost.

Even though my eyes have adapted a little, I can still only see about a footstep ahead. Enough to know I'm not walking over a cliff but that's about it. Navigating this is nearly impossible. I feel crestfallen and embarrassed. I tell myself off for being so foolhardy. I should have listened to Will, I should have listened to Jen, or at least paid attention to her raised, questioning eyebrow, something I knew meant, 'Bloody idiot, take a torch, be careful. Don't leave me alone with the kids.'

I stomp on, reckless, pig-headed and squinting. The track melts into a deer path, which leads me up a steep incline and into a dead end. I laugh and the rock laughs back, the moss-softened echo sounding manic and desperate. Cold sweat is trickling from under my hat.

I retrace my steps but manage only to lose myself further. I swear constantly. My moonlit night on the beach seems like a world away. Although I've read about the level of darkness in the pre-industrial age and the importance of the light cast by the moon and the stars, by Venus, the Shepherd's Lantern, the Morning and Evening Star, this is the first time I've really appreciated their power, have yearned for their light. I realise I have never really experienced a night that has been truly dark.

Centuries ago, when the moon was new as it is tonight, or the sky clouded, travellers had to find other ways to negotiate the murk. Embers from a torch, a white horse leading the procession, chalk left in stone of the trail or even, in woodland like this, the glimmer of a creamy axe-bite on path-side trees, would all have been ways to find a bearing. To get through and out of the night.

I keep moving. Slowly, shuffling. I can hear the sound of water, the rush of a flow over rock and wood. I've been trying to keep its flat roar at a constant level, wary of getting too close, but the noise is louder now, much louder, as if the path is directly above it. I can feel the spray on my face.

I am edgy and tense. It is the first time I've felt any-thing like the creeping chill of fear while out alone at night. I hum to myself, Simon and Garfunkel, trying to make a friend of the darkness. I try and drill down into the unease, to understand it. I don't think it's a feeling of dread, of hairs raised and marrow frozen, but more a discombobulation. A giddiness, at the way night has unbalanced my senses, heightened by the threat of fall or injury. It is odd, uncomfortable, untethered.

The last time I felt this way was when I was kayaking off the Isle of Harris. Leaving a sea loch, I was greeted by a rolling swell that left me disorientated and sick. I didn't feel just dizzy or nauseous but as if I was going to fall from the kayak. No, more than that, I felt utterly out of control, almost as if I wanted to sink into the depths.

The same is true now. With no landmarks or way of orienting myself I'm slipping down into the dark. Part choice, part fate.

I concentrate on my breathing. Feeling ridiculous that I've been reduced to a trembling mess in the dark after walking probably less than a mile. I think how other writers would have succeeded. They would have strode on bravely, accompanied by owls and badgers, pine martens and squirrels. I think about heading back, defeated, but I'm not sure I can. I don't know which way 'back' is.

The cloud breaks and through the trees there is now a patchwork, a map of night, running in velvet rivers where the shy crowns of the oaks allow each other space to grow. I can see my breath, a light curling mist, and directly under me, water. Two inky jets pulse like severed arteries around a boulder the size and shape of a gravestone. In the blackness there is the occasional lick of startling white foam.

The burn twists around, going under the rotten tree where I'm standing, before following the path back into the tree-mantled darkness. I must have been walking on the edge. I concentrate on my breathing again. I think about the advice given to those who tumble into cold water. Don't struggle, don't try to swim straight away, just float until your body adapts. While my recent experiences of the dark have been calming, the night a peaceful retreat, this is suffocating. Breathe. Breathe. I am trying to stay afloat in the night although it feels as if I'm inches away from drowning.

Even with the cloud cover breaking, the wood around me is still impenetrably black. One of the ways astronomers measure the darkness of skies is the Bortle scale: a nine-level numeric scale designed to help evaluate darkness and compare its levels at different sites, ranging from Class 1, the darkest sky on earth, through to the Class 9 of inner-city skies. The observatory at Galloway offers a night of around Class 3.

But tonight, under the trees, just a few miles away, it feels much, much darker.

I'm not sure how long it takes me to reach the clearing. Wrong turn follows wrong turn. Shins and arms left barked and bleeding. I sit down with my back against a pile of freshly cut logs and look past the wood's eye-scraping fringe towards where a few veteran Scots pines loom tall and black to the east: their canopies splayed like chewed-up, soot-clogged brushes. Between them and directly above me the stars are out. A fizz of light flowering between darkling clouds that bustle and shunt, closing one piece of the sky to open up a space elsewhere.

I have brought a planisphere, purchased from the observatory's shop, a disc that shows the positions of the stars and constellations for any hour in the year. I nearly left it behind – in my naivety I hadn't thought I'd really need it, convinced I knew what I was doing – but I'm glad to have it now. I take a guess at the time and turn the plastic discs, squinting at the small, faintly luminous digits. I hold it above my head, wobbling on the logs, try-ing to match the night of disc to the night above me. But nothing seems to fit. The clouds are shifting too quickly for me to keep up; the stars that do emerge have been bitten from their constellations.

I drink tea from my flask and look for the North Star, but without the pointer stars of the Plough, I struggle with this too. Yet, despite my frustration, seeing the stars, seeing their light, brings some comfort after the impenetrable darkness of the forest. Even fragmented, unknowable and unidentifiable, they expand the world from beyond snagging branches and darkened woods. People talk of the stars, or the heavens, as being timeless.

But sitting here it feels as if their light has more time than we can imagine. Their glow, travelling across vast distances over thousands of years, illuminates the brevity of life's guttering candle. But they are also still the same patterns of our night they have always been. A reassuring reminder that beyond these unfamiliar, isolating woods, the rest of the world is still out there, still turning as it has always done. The night no longer feels suffocating, but almost welcoming.

The relief doesn't last long. The clearing grows increasingly dark, as if the night is still rising up the hill behind me. The line of pines disappears as the clouds pack tighter. The last star is partially covered with a thin vapour trail of cloud. It glimmers and then it too has gone. A wetted finger to a wick. A smokeless snuffing.

The cloud, sky and air are one. The night shrinks around me like wet clothing. Time stops with the light.

I don't know how long I've been sitting here. It's too dark to do anything else and I don't want to move in case I lose my bearings. I know my feet, stretched out in front of me, are still pointing in the direction of the path.

I sit.

And sit.

No animals.

No thing.

Even the sound of the water doesn't flow up here.

The land holds its breath.

Sleeps.

I feel utterly alone. I'm surprised at how I am reeling without the stars, how important that connection has become. Without them, I am hanging in space waiting for creation; waiting for the shadow to lift. If the light of the stars has the power to overwhelm, to highlight both our own insignificance and the vastness of the natural world, the pitch black can swallow you whole. The darkness surrounds me. No, more than that. To be surrounded would suggest some tensile surface to strain against and puncture, but this complete absence of light is skinless, limitless, all-consuming.

Under the moon and in the snow-covered forest, I'd felt that the change in the light, the creep of darkness, had deepened my experience of the landscape. It was as if the removal of the sharpness of daylight had also taken away a barrier that had separated me from the natural world. In the darkness there was nothing between me, stone, sand, tree and deer. Yet now, with no light at all, it feels as if I'm struggling to stop myself from merging too far into the dark, from disappearing.

All I want to do is what every human who has experienced this darkness has done. I want to turn on a light, to push back against it; to illuminate the world and myself. But it feels as though even if I had a torch, its beam would not knock a hole into this blackness. The light would be swallowed, dismissed like a leaf in a flood.

Last week, I chatted with Travis Longcore, assistant professor of architecture, spatial sciences and biological sciences at the University of Southern California, who, along with Catherine Rich, compiled and edited *Ecological Consequences of Artificial Lighting*. During our conversation, conducted via the blue glow of computer screens, he had spoken about absolute darkness: its rarity, and how it exists only in truly remote places; far out to sea, in the depths of deserts.

But he also mentioned something else. Even quite a distance from cities and towns, light bounces from the clouds to create a glow in the sky. But there is also an inflection point – a magical limit where, far enough away from light, clouds act as a shield rather than a reflector, forming an impenetrable canopy that increases the darkness to levels beyond what we are used to. He described it as 'a darkness where you cannot find yourself', where visually orientated wildlife have to wait it out. Including nocturnal species that are used to operating at low light levels – those creatures with a mirror-like tapetum lucidum that reflects light back through the retina, even owls with their rod-rich eye tubes that are divining rods for voles.

I wonder if that's the night I'm in now. I came to Scotland looking for stars and darkness, but I never expected this. It is the night of the subterranean. Of cave and hole. A darkness that has risen from the earth to blot out the sky.

I can't believe the stillness. No footsteps, stirrings or even the bum-shuffles of restless pigeons. Listening to silence. A silence not of open, empty spaces, but of an earth that has seemingly emptied itself out completely. It's deep and old and disconcerting. Against it my brain feels as if it is crashing with noise, grinding its gears against itself. A hooting, honking, backfiring clamour.

I try to concentrate, to clear my mind, to quieten my thoughts, but it's no good. My blood sings, my nerves whine. The insides of my eyelids seem lighter than the outsides.

I've heard of how archaeologists and cavers have seen things, lights, while sitting in absolute darkness. Their own invisible hands become veined with blue light, the rocks themselves creeping with an impossible electric haze: cold sparks from cracks and crag. The mind filling in the dark. I wonder how long it takes to see such things. Five minutes? Five hours? Five days?

As the darkness pushes in, seeps through my skin, my brain feels as though it is going into overdrive, trying to make its own entertainment. It burrows into itself, picks at scabs. I question what I am doing, not just here, but in my life generally. The decisions made to move from Sussex to Suffolk, to give up my job. I think about conversations and conflicts from more than a decade ago, how I have wronged and been wronged, how I could and should be kinder. The thoughts spiral, until I'm no longer thinking about the darkness at all, but feeling increasingly bleak.

I cry for the first time I can remember. First without even knowing it, the tears tracing quietly down my cheeks, and then in hard, racking, snot-jerking sobs. I don't even know why I'm doing it. I laugh at myself, but still cry, the awful noise of it shaking through the woods. Perhaps I cry for the grandparents I have lost in the past few months, the stress of work, the passing of time, the worries of family life. But I think it is also for myself; pathetic and stuck in the woods.

I think again of Travis's words, about how in the dark you cannot find yourself. Yet, that is the only thing I seem to have found.

I pull myself together as the darkness lifts, enough for me to see my outstretched feet and retrace my steps through the forest and back to the car. I get in, and instinctively lock the doors. I put the radio on. Breathe. Breathe. In the rear-view mirror my face looks haunted, the skin sallow in the yellow bloom of the interior light. My eyes are dark, almost black, as if the pupils have yet to snap back. I feel hollow, as if I've been sucked inside out by the darkness, as if I've left something out there among the pine, the old oaks and wet grass.

I push in the clutch and start the engine, the headlights knifing white into the night as I drive back towards the coast. I glance at the clock. I've been sitting in the dark for three hours. It felt like a lifetime.

The road is full of man-made stars. Catseyes. The green eyes of sheep, road signs and the red reflectors of parked lorries. I pull into a layby close to the caravan park where we are staying and turn the headlights off. I want to gather myself and think. The dark rushes in as the dashboard fades.

I get out of the car and stretch, feeling my back click and pull. Stiff from the drive, stiff from tension. My jaw aches from clenching. Now that I've been released from the forest's dark grip, the clouds have gone. To the north Girvan is lit up. Pretty in the dark. The amusements, the peeling paint, the harbour with its ropes, chains and stinking creels all hidden. Above me the stars are out. More stars than I have ever seen. A swirling, textured spray that wheels from hill to sea.

The change from the utter darkness of the wood is unbelievable. The claustrophobia of an hour or so before replaced by a feeling of harmony. The night unfurled and glittering is a tapestry of stories, journeys, of almost infinite time. The joy of the stars also comes from light that is becoming more and more familiar, finally helping me to see past the discomfort I once felt. I haven't lost my sense of awe at their immense scale and beauty, but I no longer feel overwhelmed by it.

I think back to two nights ago, to how David had pointed out shapes and patterns. I can see the Summer Triangle of Deneb, Vega and Altair. I follow it to Cygnus, the Swan, the Northern Cross, its long neck stretched across the sky. There is the asterism of the Plough, the pointer stars on the edge of its saucepan, slopping milky light towards the North Star in the tail of Ursa Minor. There is the loose W of Cassiopeia: a dot-to-dot peregrine locked in a perpetual stoop towards the earth. There are colours, too. Faint but distinguishable. The cool, blue, icy-white of the hottest stars, the hot reds and oranges of the coolest.

As I climb onto the car to lie down on the bonnet, the sky begins to melt. Meteors. Candle wax drips. The stars fall at the same speed as the gannets who plunge into the sea of Ailsa Craig. It is, and there are no other words for it, truly beautiful.

This is the Perseid meteor shower, a phenomenon that appears every August as the earth passes through the trail of dust left by the comet Swift-Tuttle. Named after the constellation from which they seem to descend, each falling star, each heavenly gannet, is only the size of a grain of sand. It lights and glows as pressure builds around it, before vapourising in the atmosphere, a ghost of a comet now growing its own tail of light.

At the observatory, David had told us to look out for the Perseids. At its peak, there can be up to sixty or seventy meteors an hour. In 2016 a figure of as many as 200 an hour was recorded. Fewer appear earlier in the night but they can be more spectacular as they grow longer tails from grazing more atmosphere. They are the lights of omens, of wishes, of war, famine and hope, of gods peeking onto the mortal world. So much projection onto a mote of burning dust.

Directly above me the Milky Way cracks the blackness of the sky, even clearer than it was at the observatory. The arm of our own galaxy swinging through space.

Another meteor drops. Then another, the trail lasting longer this time, a hint of green, yellow, red. Light really does have power. I feel joyous, alive, part of something gigantic and wonderful. But I want to share it, I don't want to experience this alone.

I wake Jen as I fumble the lock on the caravan and lead her bleary-eyed to the balcony. More stars melt from the sky and I point proudly up at the smudge of the Milky Way, as if I had provided all this for her. She leans smiling against the frame of the sliding door, wrapped in a thick white dressing gown, letting only her face feel the cool of the night. She looks up at the froth of stars, the river of gas.

'Gosh, it is gorgeous.'

I decide to get the kids up too. Seth is fast asleep. I smooth away a curl from his forehead and kiss him, smelling the chlorine from a day of playing in the pool, the sweetness of his breath. 'I just want to sleep, Dad.'

I try Eliza in the next room. I hold her hand and ask if she wants to see a shooting star. She growls something and turns over, hugging the duvet and sticking her head deep into a mound of cuddly toys. Next to her bed are a pile of books, open and face down. On top rests the planisphere I bought the children, hoping to ignite an interest in the night skies. I can see it has been set to today's date, they must have been looking while I was out. So what if they miss the meteor shower tonight? The children have a lifetime of stars ahead of them. Maybe they'll try to show their own kids the stars one day, an inspiration of light that set off on its journey this very night.

I go back outside. Jen has made her escape and padded back to bed, so I sit alone on a cold, plastic chair and draw a blanket over my legs. After such an emotional night, I suddenly feel at peace. Sometimes it's best to stay still and let the darkness find you. Let the turn of the earth do the work.

Another shooting star, this time a ground burner, flies horizontally across the sky from south to north. 'Ooooh,' I shout. 'Wonderful!'

There's a *whoomp* and a click as Jen pushes the patio door behind me closed. I look at her and she smiles sleepily, raising a finger to her lips and then blowing me a kiss.

'Ooooh,' I whisper.

3

Night Terrors

A cuckoo is calling from the haunted heart of Wistman's Wood. Shouting his own name between the wind-stunted, gnarled and knotted oaks. He is flushed into a clearing, chased by another bird, to settle, hawkish, on a moss-covered branch.

I clamber down onto a slab of rock and look into the valley: over the trees, with their clitter-guarded roots and the deep reek of age, down to the thin, tin-coloured flow of the West Dart and the tor behind it. Somewhere a cock is crowing. The sound is funnelled and carried by the steepness of the river's cut. Strained through the wood. This time of day was once known as cock-shut. A time to go inside and batten the doors, for the night will soon stalk the world on shadowy limbs. When even the locals are said to avoid coming up here, across bog and mire, to the gloaming wood.

Bad things happen out on the moor.

After being reduced to tears in Scotland, I've been dwelling on night fear. While I know that for me the experience was unusual, one of unsettling strangeness, fear of the dark is certainly not unusual. Whenever I mention I've been for a walk at night, friends generally respond in the same way. Alone? Weren't you scared? Rather you than me. What is it about the night that provokes such dread?

The absence of light is clearly a factor, the disorientation of twilight as our eyes switch from cones to rods, reducing our ability to pick out colour and detail, increasing the sharpness of other senses. Faced with the dark, we cling to light to soothe our fears. The child's nightlight brings comfort; it stands watch against the darkness while parents sleep. But light, whether artificial or natural, can only push back the night so far. The shadows still lurk, holding unmentionable terrors until dawn finally chases them away.

Writing in the seventeenth century, John Locke claimed fear of the dark originated in tales told to wide-eyed children; stories of 'raw-head and bloody-bones, and such other names as carry with them the ideas of something terrible and hurtful, which they have reason to be afraid of when alone, especially in the dark'.

Once such ideas have entered into the 'tender minds' of children, he said, they are hard to dislodge, 'making children dastards when alone, and afraid of their shadows and darkness all their lives after'.

It is certainly an instinct most children have experienced. Night was probably my first terror. I remember, when I was too small to reach light switches, I would leave the brightly lit front room, with its TV chatter and my parents, to go and retrieve a favourite toy, a stuffed monkey. I would count as I went. Ten to get to and scramble up the stairs, ten to cross the darkened landing and bolt in and out of my room and then ten more to safety.

Don't look back, never look back.

The dark reached into my dreams too. I used to have a recurring nightmare in which the darkness was like a mist filling the empty house. I would float above it, inches off the floor, and although I turned on the lights, the bulbs always proved to be unnaturally dim. They flickered over swirling shadows that would eventually rise over my feet, shins and knees, the air suddenly thick and noxious. It was hard to breathe, let alone shout out. Not that anyone would hear.

Night is, in our collective consciousness, a time of fear and trembling. The word 'nightfall' itself is rooted in death; the diminishing light was once thought to bring with it a poisonous haze. In the fifteenth century it was commonly held that these vapours contributed to the darkness just as much as the lowering sun. Night drop was a cloud of clotted air that entered the skin, addled organs and brought pain, fever and death. In Shakespeare's *Measure for Measure*, the Duke warns Mariana to 'make haste; the vaporous night approaches'.[3] Thomas Dekker, an Elizabethan pamphleteer, described the airs of darkness as 'that thick tobacco-breath which the rheumatic night throws abroad'.[4] Windows were closed against the night, the lack of ventilation no doubt helping to spread whatever illness the dark-fearing patient held.

Fear of the dark is bound up in religion too. The darkness of night is ever-present in the Bible, as a natural, ready-made domain to be shaped and moulded to invoke fear and spur obedience. Darkness smokes from the pages, sulphur-scented, clotting the air. Created by God (Genesis 1:5), darkness sits in opposition to his light, both as a metaphor for evil and a literal description of those who dwell in the shadows. To go into the darkness of night, to eschew the day, was to take part in orgies and drunkenness, sexual immorality and sensuality, quarrelling and jealousy (Romans 13:13). The dark of night is where sinners are thrown, whether fallen angel or bad servant; it is a place where there will be much 'weeping and gnashing of teeth' (Matthew 22:13). Satan, that prince of darkness, was held responsible for all of the supernatural activities of the night. Accompanied by legions of witches – which kissed his rump in sexually charged nocturnal Sabbaths and who had the power to kill livestock, shrivel limbs and 'bewitch' male genitalia – the black of night was the devil's time to shape the earth.

But is fear of the dark something we learn or something we're born with? Perhaps our primitive fear of night is an evolutionary residue of times when the landscape was dangerous. When tooth and claw could turn the blackness blood red. The aversion to night part of a survival instinct hard-wired into the human brain, kindling an innate fear. Perhaps it is an ancient, shared memory of an awful predator, a creature that could have attacked early humans as they sheltered in cave entrances, dragging them deeper into the dark caverns to strip flesh and devour. Could it be that this terror lingers, abstracted and transformed into different shapes? An inherited fear that has morphed into the haunting concept of evil.

The philosopher Edmund Burke certainly felt the fear of night was too universal, too old, to be purely the result of scary stories in childhood. He instead suggested that the terrible dread of darkness comes from the fact that within its shadows it is impossible to know 'in what degree of safety we stand; we are ignorant of the objects that surround us'. It is because the night is a place of fear and the unknown that we find it a suitable place for the malevolent and monstrous, rather than the other way around. We yearn for the sun to return, banishing the horrors that live in the dark, bringing with it relief, reassurance, safety. And, until it does, we seek temporary comfort in whatever light we can find.

For the best part of the day I've been walking along the Lych Way, a trail that winds across the moors and tors of north Dartmoor. Those who dwelled in the ancient tenements and villages would have followed this route to attend church in the parish of Lydford. It was also the path they trod to carry their dead, until a new church was built late in the 1200s.

The route, over hill and through sunken, cloistered holloways, is littered with reminders of ancient passings. Near Conies Down, the wheel ruts of corpse wagons are still visible, and letterboxes along the route have been decorated with coffins, crosses and skeletons. The Lych Way is also known as the Corpse Way. It is the Way of the Dead.

I don't have much further to go. Wistman's Wood is just four or five miles from where I started out late this morning and I'm determined to complete the last leg at night.

When it comes to thinking about the night as a place of bleakness, of spookiness, of the supernatural, Dartmoor seemed like a good place to come. While Exmoor nearby has been designated as a Dark Sky Reserve, the nights of its southerly neighbour are also relatively free from the orange blush of light pollution. But more fittingly, it is hard to think of a landscape with as many tales of terror as Dartmoor. Its moors, bogs, tors and woods teem with them. They well from the dark earth and howl from its valleys. Nearly all the rocks of the tors – teetering scatological plops scoured by ice creep, freeze and thaw – have backstories and associations with spirits and gods that emerge at night. Sometimes even the rocks themselves are said to dance with the moonlight.

The roads are haunted too. The stretch between Postbridge and Two Bridges – a route I drove this morning – is supposedly terrorised by a pair of disembodied hands, sometimes invisible, sometimes hairy. They are said to have grabbed at steering wheels and handlebars, forcing nocturnal travellers from the road.

Peter Ackroyd, in his book *The English Ghost: Spectres Through Time*, suggests there are more than 200 ways of describing the supernatural creatures that lurk in places of nocturnal darkness. They form an unwholesome clamour of apparitions, shades, phantoms, phantasms, manes, visitants, fetches, scrags, larrs, ouphs, swathes, scarbugs, nickies, bolls, gringes, freits, chittifaces, tokens, frittenins and spoorns. Not to forget, the fantastically named clabbernappers and mum-pokers.

The fact that places that are inhospitable, uninhabited or abandoned are often home to ghosts and spirits is surely not coincidence. Marsh, mere, bog and swamp are all old words that attest to the restlessness of the landscape, its capacity to shift and change, to swallow and kill. At night we feel the uneasiness of the land and we can't help but fear it.

These areas of our countryside often remain dark; full of pitfalls, ditches and streams. Many stories of night terror no doubt come from stumbles and accidents. But fear, sharpened by confused and limited senses, lends missteps and mistakes a ghoulish air.

As I arrive at the northern edge of Wistman's Wood, I

can see why the stories here are thicker than the sun-shy moss that corsets every shrivelled trunk. Each wizened oak is rooted in tales of druid worship, ghosts, the devil and the old gods. It is here that the Wisht Hounds are said to be kennelled: the bloodthirsty, soul-hungry dogs of the dark huntsman – thought by some to be the devil, while others claim he is the spirit of the moor itself. Whisper his name and he will come. Old Crockern, a protective and vengeful force that patrols Dartmoor on a skeletal steed; his face granite grey, his eyes as black as the darkest peat pools.

Before I came here I had read a collection of songs written by Edward Capern as he completed his rounds as a rural postman in 1865 and one in particular stuck with me. It is a gruesome story of a farmer who, with whisky in his belly and sleep in his eyes, encountered the spectral hunt as he returned from market. After asking for some of the huntsman's game, he was tossed a package that was too small for a deer and too large for a hare. He unwrapped it at home to find the body of his unbaptised son. The tale takes place on a night devoid of light:

Oh, for a wild and starless night,
And a curtain o'er the white moon's face,
For the moor fiend hunts an infant sprite.

The hounds are said to swallow light itself, the hair on their hides so black it repels starlight and torchlight, their sulphurous breath turning reflective streams to stinking mires and their blood-curdling howls stopping the hearts of ordinary dogs. The Wisht Hounds supposedly inspired Sir Arthur Conan Doyle's Hound of the Baskervilles. It is their terror and the fear of night-soaked Dartmoor that Hugo Baskerville conjures when he warns, 'I counsel you by way of caution to forbear from crossing the moor in those dark hours when the powers of evil are exalted.'

Not only am I ignoring his warning, my route is taking me straight into their lair. From my rocky seat I gaze deeper into the wood, at the writhing pygmy oaks dripping with low light and even lower lichen. I have never seen trees grow like this. They have schemed their way out of the ground, contorting and twisting into bizarre lightning-strike shapes, the boughs snaking and dipping.

Much has been written about Wistman's, its magic and links to Druids, its beauty, its romance. But it has also challenged and scared. In 1797, the artist and topographer the Reverend John Swete said, 'It is hardly possible to conceive any thing of the sort so grotesque as this Wood appears.'

In the last fading rays of the light, I can see why so many find this place unsettling. Wistman's is of another time, a place of eldritch darkness. A scrap of old wood from which night never really retreats.

I must have nodded off. The sun is gone, and the skylarks that connected sky to moor with scribbles of song have dropped to earth. Darkness has risen, stilling even the light breath of wind that had moved over the tors.

A sheep calls for her lambs, a dark shape against the dark rocks behind me, and a pony, somewhere on the moor, lets out a banshee scream. The woods crouch in their steep cut, ominous yet, for the moment, devil- and Crockern-free. I get up, my back corpse-cold from the granite slab, put on my shirt and stiffly shoulder my pack. It's time to move.

In the daylight, I felt pretty sure of my route, but now there is a creep of uncertainty, and memories of the woods in Scotland only add to my unease. I turn from the trees and climb the steep slope that leads up to Littaford Tor to get a better view. The early night sky is clear and sloe-coloured, with the first stars appearing like the scattered lights of a distant hamlet. It is a world away from the cloud-shrouded darkness of Scotland, when tales of terror might have pushed me over the edge. My confidence returns, boosted by the starlight. The night feels calm and peaceful. Its coolness a tonic after the skin-tightening heat of day. Even though the moon, late to bed, is still to rise, visibility is not bad. Dartmoor spreads out beneath me. The detail of day reduced to a landscape of base elements. Earth, rock, sky. Highland and lowland.

I start to walk, weaving between rocks. Moths, disturbed by my footfall, flit, wood-shaving pale around my legs. There is no choice but to go slow, especially on ground this uneven. If the Wisht Hounds were to chase me tonight, there would be no hope of outrunning them. Any increase in speed would lead me to turn an ankle or roll over granite rocks that cascade down into a bowl-like cut in the moor.

I stick close to a drystone wall where the ground, if not flat, doesn't seem too boggy. I wonder if I'm also subconsciously seeking its protection, avoiding being too exposed, but quickly dismiss the idea before it can take root and make me feel on edge again.

In the end, it is not Crockern that catches me but a loop of barbed wire, invisible against the stonework. I scrape my arm and jump, which causes me to slip and plant my left foot in a stream partially hidden by long strands of mat grass. My boot and lower leg are sodden. I swear noisily, the loudness of my own voice startling both me and a soot-coloured pony that ambles off on bog-sucking hooves. I wonder if it's the banshee I heard before. A taste of his own medicine.

While not scared about being here in the dark, alone, I am certainly not relaxed. It is a sense of heightened awareness, a highly strung readiness. I wonder how easily it could be tipped into fear. As the twilights melt into night and the darkness grows, all my senses are reaching out, grasping any stimuli they can find as I walk in a small tunnel of reduced visibility, lit only by the pinprick light of the first stars and the lichen, which radiates softly from rocks. I move my head constantly to give my eyes a chance to pick out detail, I touch everything, skimming stones and grass with outstretched fingers. I sniff and snortle at the night. Despite the coolness of the air, I am sweating with the effort of it all.

It's not the idea of the hounds or other supernatural beings that is unnerving me right now, rather the simple worry of getting lost. In Scotland, in the black tangle of trees, I became disorientated so easily. The experience seems to have left its mark. I thought being out in the open like this would help, but I feel just as vulnerable, a roving spot in a dark expanse that stretches for miles. I am not known for my sense of direction, but in the daytime it's fairly simple to find the way again, to pick out guiding details in the landscape. Darkness, though, turns you around, flattens the colours and features of your world, robs you of your confidence. Maybe we are not used to being truly lost, lightless and alone.

In the lower moor the cows have also been making use of the Lych Way. Their movements (and their copious excretions) have reduced the path to a sticky mire. Despite almost two months of solid sun there is still water here, welling from peat and bog, making it almost impossible to walk. I'm forced to change my route, swinging right into tussocks and firmer ground.

I step. Jump between humps of grass. Follow the bright, fleecy lights of cotton sedge, which seems almost luminescent against the darkness of the earth. But this plant is also known as bog cotton. Its light is a will-o'-the-wisp leading me into the deep, dank heart of the marsh. First there is a warning squelch, and then with the next hop into the dark, both legs disappear up to my thigh. The water is cold, squid-ink black. The earth under it, gripping tight. Pulling. Holding.

I panic and thrash, thinking about tales of night-time falls and drownings, how Jen will kill me if I don't make it back. But I'm not sinking deeper. I lean back. Limboing towards firmer ground. I extract one leg and then the other, before lying there, panting.

I fish down into the bog to find my boot – sucked off as I extracted myself – and check the rest of my gear. Everything is there. Smeared with black mud, wet and cold. My legs are soaked to the groin, my trousers now *Rocky Horror Show* stockings. I must look like something of the night.

The trail leads north-west, through the wall and onto drier land, where I can hear a stream behind a thicket of scrawny-looking trees. To the left is the remains of a building and the grey stone finger of an old gunpowder mill. The roofless buildings echo the tumbledown jumble of the tor, its chimney now home to rooks. One takes flight while another remains inside, its croaky *what, what, what* amplified by the flue. It is an eerie noise; a haunting. Particularly when you can't see the source.

I wonder how much of our fear must come from the reduction of our vision, our eyes and minds playing tricks on us. The eye fills with darkness. Without the most treasured of senses, the heart of our perceptual world, we are, or at least feel, blinkered. Grasping in the dark among a world of unnamed sounds is no substitute for the clarity of sight, the safety of the known. Imagination, especially if we are lost and panicking, fills in the gaps with terrifying detail: a Goya-esque vision of depravity, death and eerily animated bog gas.

Even light can't always be trusted when fear and an overactive mind take hold. The dark nights of the pre-industrial age were alive with strange lights, orbs and bright mists that lured people into perilous bog and marsh. They were fairy lights or the Devil's lantern. Elemental spirits, known by the charming name of spunkie in the Highlands, which receded when approached, as if urging the traveller to follow. The light is a common theme. We trust it, we want it, we walk towards it.

Modern science has explained will-o'-the-wisps by way of bioluminescence or chemiluminescence (the production of light from a chemical reaction) caused by the oxidation of gasses brought about by organic decay. The movement of the ghostly light a result of agitation of the air. But, again, it is an insight into how at night we are ready to jump from the partly seen and the not understood to fear.

Tiredness also has a role in fear born of confusion, while others who experienced the undead – just like the moorman who encountered the dark hunter – were under the influence of alcohol. Not only does alcohol impair judgement, reduce coordination and slow reaction time, it has an impact on night vision. A study carried out at the University of Grenada showed that increases in breath alcohol-content level corresponded to greater visual disturbance: the ethanol causing part of the tear film on the outer eye to evaporate.[5]

There are many synonyms for drunkenness that relate to night-time travel. In 1736, a newspaper in New England (for some unknown reason) attempted to list every term for being under the influence: 'He sees two moons'; 'Knows not the way home'.[6]

The fearful, the frightened, are not only pixy-led but pished.

I am close to the edge of the moor, in sight of the road that separates bog from forest, when I hear them. A cold engine refusing to turn over, a bubbling, pneumatic drilling. The song comes from nowhere and everywhere, bouncing from the spindle-sharp pines of the plantation, drifting over to reach me in pulsing, clicking churrs of 1,900 notes a minute. Spokie dokies on a child's bike. Mechanical, like an over-wound toy. The nightjars are here.

The last time I heard nightjars was in the same place I had my first night walk, the King's Forest near my home in Bury St Edmunds, last summer. It was also the first time I had actually seen a nightjar, had watched it circle in a paper-plane glide, tail up and kestrel-shaped wings glowing with a mineral flash of white. Time and time again he had flown over me, clapping his wings together over his back like an airborne flamenco dancer; each slap of feathered bone the click of a castanet.

I stand on a granite slab and cup my hands to my ears to try to work out where the birds are. I turn slowly, counting: one, two, three different calls. A cicada song of summer heat. And, like seeing the stars, identifying a familiar sound in the night brings joy, providing a brief anchoring point in the dark, wide expanse of Dartmoor.

Nightjars, because of the hours they keep and their curious beauty – bark-coloured bodies, sphinx-like head and wide, whisker-fringed, moth-funnelling gape – have long been shrouded in myth. For centuries it was believed the bird suckled on goats, leaving any animal they visited blind, its precious milk forever soured. The folklore of the goat-sucker is echoed in the nightjar's Latin name, *Caprimulgus europaeus*, 'milker of goats'.

As with tales of night-loving witches in the Early Modern Age, any illness that befell livestock would also be blamed on the nightjar, whose proximity to animals was actually due to the associated insects, rather than a desire for milk or mischief. Cows, too, were said to be 'victims' of the nightjars' feeds. In some regions the bird is known as 'Puckeridge' after the disease it supposedly caused in cattle by pecking at hides.

Appropriately enough for where I am now, the nightjar was also known as the 'Lich fowl'. The corpse bird. Born not from eggs but the souls of unbaptised children, doomed to fly through the night until Judgement Day.

By the time I leave them and cross the road to the wood, the moon, waning away from last quarter, is starting to rise. But I won't benefit from its light in the forest. I walked here this morning when the shade of the trees had been welcoming. I had sat with my back against a pine and drunk tea, read a book. It's the same forest, but it couldn't feel more different. The wood blocks out almost everything else. The dark floods out from trees that push up tight against a path that now seems not much wider than a couple of feet. Not big enough for a funeral cart. Not enough room to swing a corpse. I feel more on edge than I did either at Wistman's or out on the open hound-stalked moor. I become startled by the sound of my own backpack, the movement on the peripheries. The hooked, dead man's fingers of the fir.

I stop and pick twigs from the caked mud of my trousers, still not dry from my bog dip. My legs feel heavy, tired no doubt from a day of walking, weighed down with swamp-grot and cold. I look back at the moor and wish I hadn't. The way forward looks so much darker. I shiver. Never look back, never look back.

I am walking faster than I have all night. But it's the worst thing to do. Adrenalin starts to surge. My chest tightening, the breaths quicker and shallow. The more I move my head, the more I see, or think I see, among the trees' treacling shadows.

I had thought I was immune to this, that my fears were reasonable, logical, based solely on the practical concern of getting lost. But perhaps I was wrong. It's all I can do to keep my pace level, to stop myself from running. I know if I did, the fear would only grow – I would be in flight from something unseen. The primitive fear of the night and unseen monsters lurking in the shadows would kick in and take over.

Deeper into the forest are the remains of a bonfire. Three large logs half eaten by flame. Around them are scattered crisp packets and fag ends. A beer can, crushed, is half shoved under an exposed tree root. In the daytime the discovery wouldn't have been much of a surprise. Tut-worthy, the most severe of British admonishments.

But now it feels strange, unnerving, that there might be other people here, unseen, their purpose unknown.

Why bother to populate the night with imaginary monsters when there are plenty of more tangible terrors around? Real villains and real crimes have had a long association with the night both in towns and the countryside. Night was a means of cover for thieves and robbers, who, during the pre-industrial period (and probably still now) were considered to be nocturnal in nature. They 'sleepeth by daye' so they 'may steale by night'.[7]

During those times when the tatler moon was hidden, thieves were known to have tripped their victims by stretching ropes across darkened, narrow streets, while in rural regions, so-called low-pads used long poles to dismount those on horseback. Burglars waited for households to be asleep, for the 'cull to be at snoos', before breaking in. 'Smudges' and 'night-sneaks' would find a way to enter during the day to hide beneath beds. Some gangs were known to have cut through walls of wattle and daub or wormed their way through roofs. The snuffing of candles, the putting out of lights, was a sign to the watching criminal that his hour had almost come.

Back then, it was in the seasons when the night was darkest, between autumn and spring, when crime was thought to take hold. While the dark itself disguised identity, the criminally intent also wore other disguises – long cloaks, masks, hats – and carried 'dark lanterns' where light was emitted from only one side. The victims' own lights would be put out, leaving them trembling and senseless in the dark.

The supernatural and the superbad also worked together. Although the footpads and thugs of the Early Modern Age were understood to be human, they still had magical associations. Moonwort, whose fan-shaped leaves resemble a half-moon, was thought by thieves to open locks, as was mandrake – a plant that was believed to grow under the gallows when urine or blood from the condemned touched the ground.

The most famous magical tool was probably 'the thief's candle', made from an amputated human finger, taken from an executed criminal or an unbaptised child. The gruesome, guttering, oily light the candle produced was said to keep the family of a burglarised home deep in sleep.

The night not only protected criminals, it made them. The darkness, the disguises it provided, meant that social boundaries could be crossed. Matthew Beaumont describes in his book *Nightwalking* how it was not uncommon for aristocrats to 'roister around London after dark'. An assortment of bloods, bucks, blades, gallants and roarers embraced the night as part of a libertine life, a time of freedom where they could descend the social ladder to run amok: fighting, gambling and destroying property.

Throughout different periods, stories of well-born, well-heeled gangs – the Damned Crew, the Muns, the Tityré Tūs, the Hectors, the Scourers, the Nickers, and the Hawkubites – caused terror in London. In the eighteenth century one aristocratic gang, the Mohocks, were said to knife pedestrians in the face and sexually assault women. According to one Lady Wentworth, 'They put an old woman into a hogshead, and rolled her down a hill; they cut off some noses, others' hands, and several barbarous tricks, without any provocation. They are said to be young gentlemen; they never take any money from any.'

Hard evidence of such an organised gang is scant, but there were plenty of lurid accounts written at the time, so it seems people were certainly willing to believe they existed. Perhaps we're determined to populate the night with monsters, real or imagined – or maybe just a little exaggerated – to justify our fear of it. If darkness makes us tremble, our brains must provide a reason why, to make sense of the things we half see in the dim light, to transform the unusual bounce of moonlight at the edge of our vision into figures, the deep shadows into monstrous forms that only light can chase away.

I set off again, keeping my speed steady, concentrating on each step, the rolling heel-to-toe rhythm of walking. The track opens again, leading through a rough patch of heathy moor with the piled, paving-stone peak of Bellever Tor to the right, before heading back into the mantling dark of the wood. After half an hour I begin to realise that I should be out of the forest by now. The rides seem to be endless.

Distracted by my fear of the unseen, my original fear has been realised. I'm lost.

I'm calmer than I thought I'd be. Somehow it seems easier to deal with this concrete problem than the imaginary ones haunting my peripheral vision.

I consider retracing my steps or just pulling out my bivvy bag and sleeping, but instead decide to push on. Out of the darkness I see a fox. Its tread perfect, the rear pad swapping places with the forefoot in a hypnotic, rhythmic trot. Its colour is not readily visible in the dark, instead its coat looks very grey or black, even its full brush seems to be lacking its white tip. I follow it from a distance as it hurries along the track. Occasionally it stops, looks over its shoulder and then jogs on again.

It knows I'm here, it must do, everything about it is better suited for the night than I am. The fox pauses once more, then jinks left to a gate and a road. I hear the clip of claw on tarmac and then it's gone.

The myth of foxes in Dartmoor is strong. They were once considered 'devil's spies' on the hunt for souls. A fox, a 'hector', crossing the path was a bad omen. Yet, I am mightily glad to have seen this one. It has led me out of the woods.

A sign by the roadside suggests I have come a good two miles out of the way. If I'm to get back to the car before dawn I've either got to go back into the forest or follow the sign along the road, definitely the longer route.

I look at the wood, its spiky blackness, an aura of darkness lying on the trees as if it is sucking in and condensing the night. I take a step back towards it before turning on my heel and striding off down the road under a star-studded sky and the faint white smudge of the Milky Way.

4

Burning Bright

From the train window I can see the moon. It was just rising as I left, clambering over rooftops and roads. Almost too bright to look at. A waxing gibbous, fat with light. The Harvest Moon swelling as the earth edges towards autumn. I can see Mars a stone's throw away. A tiny, steady candle. A dull fag-end of red light.

The moon glides west along the tracks, appearing above stations and tree lines: ghosting over the hard, flat darkness of the fens and the glare of town street-lights. Occasionally she disappears altogether, leaving windows of pure black, the brightness of the carriage meaning nothing is visible but the reflection of my own face. We are a tube of bad light and bad air, slicing through the changing twilights, carrying musty, glass-wool seats, yesterday's newspapers, empty beer cans and the stale coffee breath of the man in the seat opposite.

My friend Shaun joins me near Cambridge. He's dressed for a night on the town. Suited and booted. Smart and sharp in contrast to my grubby jeans and lumberjack jacket.

He says he didn't really know what to wear. I know what he means. If Jen hadn't intervened on my way out of the door my bag would still be full of the usual gear that I take on my countryside wanders: fire-lighting kit, fuel blocks, compass, knife.

I'm bound for London to spend the night in a city – where darkness has been banished by a constant flood of artificial light. The ultimate human triumph over the night. Now that I've had the opportunity to appreciate the different experiences of natural light, I want to examine how the night feels in a place where it's been pushed back. I want to see if in among the people, the buildings and the glare of a city that is one of the most artificially lit places on the planet, any trace of night's soft shade remains.

It's gone 11 p.m. when we leave Liverpool Street station and start to follow the route of the old London Wall. It feels like a good starting point. This is a place that was once the night's frontier. Somewhere that rang with the sound of the curfew bell. One hundred rings tolling an hour or so after sunset. Be within or be without.

Curfews in urban areas were once common across England and the rest of western Europe. Roger Ekirch suggests in his history of night *At Day's Close* that it was William the Conqueror who first imposed a national curfew of 8 p.m. in 1068. Not only were people to be inside the walls and inside their homes, but all lights had to be out. 'Curfew' itself derives from the French *couvre-feu*. Literally, 'cover fire'. It's possible that the new Norman king might have wanted to prevent the spread of fires, a common threat at a time when most heat and light came from open flames, yet it's likely the policy was also political; to prevent shadowy figures fanning the flames of nocturnal rebellion.

For centuries going out at night in towns and cities was a radical act with only a few – midwives, doctors and priests – given dispensation to roam a dark that was as deep in pitch as anywhere in the countryside. In some cities, most famously Nuremburg, the streets themselves were dressed in heavy chains to prevent walkers or carriages from moving.

In 1285 Edward I introduced the Statute of Winchester, or Statute of Winton, in response to increasing levels of crime; it stated that 'every walled town should close its gates from sunset to sunrise'.[8] A nightwatch system was formalised, with 'watch men' given the power to arrest those wandering at night and deliver them to the sheriff.

It was during the eighteenth century that things really began to change in Britain's cities. The night was slowly being illuminated, at first not so much by light as by the spread of scientific rationalism. Across an industrialised world, which increasingly questioned the teachings of the Church, the night of ghosts, of witches, of devils and child-killing wraiths was slowly exorcised. Reason and its handmaiden scepticism, according to one

London newspaper in 1788, had left the capital without a single haunted house.[9]

The night still had its dangers but with fear of the supernatural on the decline, increasingly it was becoming a time for people, especially the middle classes, to venture out. Shops and markets started to keep later hours, while mills and foundries worked long into the night. Improved roads and canalised rivers allowed livestock, goods and people to travel at any hour. Night was slowly becoming less distinct from day.

After the train journey it feels good to be out, to be free to unwind our legs, even if the brightness of it all is a shock. The roads and buildings of Old London Wall are now largely empty of people but full of light, the energy both wasteful and polluting. In the ground floors of some of the offices, banks, investment specialists, a few security guards sit at desks among modern art and uncomfortable-looking furniture worth more than my annual income. White shirt, black tie, white light.

The upper levels are also blazing. Light pools on desks laden with dual screens, runs over empty chairs, umbrella stands, water coolers, beanbags and yoga balls and glares out onto the street. Like hot sugar, it sticks to everything. I find it hard to see where one light begins and another ends.

The headlights of passing cars and couriers illuminate almost nothing. Their light is another skin on illuminated concrete and glass. All fuses with a sky that is fuzzed and blurred. What should be black is bleached to a murky burnt orange that is hardly a colour at all. The night, the darkness, seems to live only in the cracks of the pavement.

Yet these lights, alongside traditional factors such as cathedrals, universities, population size and royal assent, are an essential part of what defines a city. A city's illuminations are a proud marker of civilisation, an indication that our dependency on nature, and the daily and seasonal cycles we associate with the countryside, has been ruptured or surpassed. The geographer Yi-Fu Tuan said the village and the city are opposite ends of living with nature. At one end, 'we have the village subordinate to nature; at the other, the city that does not know how it is fed, that comes alive with winter and slights the course of the sun'.[10] While that is not necessarily true of all villages everywhere, some forty years later it is still urban areas that step furthest outside the confines of nature's cycles.

The history of light is the history of civilisation. First there was flame from knocked flints, from wood rubbed on wood, lamps made from stone and shell. Crude lights made way for Roman beeswax candles that burned so evenly they could slice the night into definite hours. Yet, for centuries most people relied on candles made from fat and oil. The bodies of cows, sheep, bears, bison, alligators and manatees were all rendered for fuel.

People made use of what was close to hand. Rushes plucked from marsh and swamp were peeled by children and dipped into fat, giving off a brittle light that Dickens described in *Great Expectations* as being 'like the ghost of a walking cane'.

In the West Indies, the Caribbean and parts of Asia, fireflies were captured and placed in cages, or glued to toes. On the coasts of Canada, salmon were skewered and burned. Shetlanders relied on storm petrels – birds famous for coming to shore at night to breed were captured in their thousands, their oily carcasses mounted on bases of clay, their throats threaded with wicks and set alight.

The places where humans lived glimmered. But it was in the nineteenth century that cities really started to conquer the night with their lights. The arrival of gas lamps in 1807 led to the first effective street lighting in London, and electricity soon followed. Experiments with arc lights, so powerful that they had to be raised above sightlines on 'moonlight towers' or suspended above streets, woke birds. The *Gazette de France* reported in 1855 that ladies opened umbrellas 'in order to protect themselves from the rays of the mysterious new sun'.[11]

Although arc lights, too unreliable and too harsh, never really caught on, they gave people a taste of brightness, of how night could be chased away. The first incandescent bulbs on a street in Britain were switched on in Newcastle upon Tyne in 1879. Then, a year later, the first market to be lit was here in London. The clue in its name: Electric Avenue.

The streets grew rowdier, busier. The wedge between the city of light and the dark countryside widened. The seasonal rhythms of rural and town life no longer matched. As the days shortened in winter, the people of villages and hamlets retreated to rooms heated by fire and still illuminated with tallow and reed light. Yet the city, wrenching itself free from the limitations of a night lit only by the moon and stars, was coming alive.

The arrival of light was not universally welcomed. While many saw a connection between the decrease of darkness and an increase in safety, others thought it would encourage anti-social behaviour. The editorial of a Cologne newspaper in 1816 argued that if the fear of the dark was removed, drunkenness and depravity would soon arrive. Perhaps there is some truth to it. The nightlife of London certainly feels hedonistic, a celebration of illicit entertainment. And however bright the lights are, however clearly we can be seen or recognised, night seems to sanction certain activities that might be seen as unacceptable in the daytime. The night is a time to misbehave.

Under the streetlights and the glare of shopfronts, the city is swaggering and staggering into the night before us. There is laughter and shouts. The pissed up and the pissed off. A girl sits with her head between her legs, crying while her friends gather round. They hold her bag, stroke her back and phone a cab. Two or three others stand a little further away, their arms crossed, eager to get going.

'Bloody hell, she always does this.'

Across the road a man, half hidden by the entrance column of a bank, is noisily sick. He emerges, pale and sheepish, to cheers. He wipes his mouth and high-fives his friends.

We follow the crowds. Run with the bellowing, shambling herd. No longer navigating by natural light, but pulled by movement, sound and neon. We veer off into Soho. If city life means nightlife, nightlife means Soho. Its very name conjures up bars and theatre, colour and light. And, of course, that other constant of the night, sex, given a soft red light of its very own.

For 200 years this one square mile of bustle and noise, bounded by Oxford Street, Regent Street, Leicester Square and Charing Cross Road, has been at the heart of the capital's nightlife. When I first came to London without my parents as a young teen, I always headed straight for Soho. Romanced by its faded glamour, its illicitness and edge. It seemed to represent a world that was completely at odds with my own. But I've never seen it like this. Soho, the old showgirl, has blinked awake and is putting on her slap.

On the main streets, now thick with people, the lights burn away the grime of day. Signs for clubs, pubs and restaurants are a riot of neon and white. People now walk slowly, spilling from taxis to queues for clubs, while the more glamorous are ushered directly in by security staff. I catch the eye of one of the bouncers. He looks at my scuffed boots and plaid jacket and gives me a 'don't even try getting in here' glare.

Although the rise of artificial light is linked, historically, with a repression of bad behaviour – the early lamps of English cities were often maintained by the police and known as 'police lamps' – there lingers a sense of the old social freedom. A time when it was light enough to go out, but dark enough to not be recognised or judged, whatever your social standing. The perpetual twilight of the lit night is a border, a hazy no man's land, between freedom and civility. And it is, for the most part, fun.

It's hard not to get caught up in the atmosphere. To soak up a feeling of people cut loose from daytime responsibilities, the office drudge, the school run; a class-less, genderless, raceless mass of humanity. Bright and bold.

We chat and laugh with those waiting to get into clubs and those leaving, refusing nips from hipflasks and offers of fags. Shaun joins a queue for one of the open-air urinals that rise from the streets with the dark and shouts over his shoulder for me to take a picture. One for the family album.

In a narrow, beige corridor behind an open door a woman sitting on a plastic fold-up chair looks at me and points upstairs. She looks fed-up and tired. I smile and shake my head. I do want to talk to her, to ask her about her nights in London, but it doesn't seem right. It feels condescending. Having to deal with lagered-up sex tourists is bad enough without being grilled by some middle-class twonk with a Thermos and a compass.

Other massage parlours are less subtle. Men sit in glass-fronted waiting rooms, reading the paper or playing with their phones. I'm surprised by it. I suppose I always thought of Soho as more of a nudge-nudge wink-wink kind of place. A seaside-postcard sauciness. This is overt. Forceful. Of course, I'm being naive. After all, in some ways this is the old night of London. Yes, the lights might be brighter, but it's still the same lure of booze and sex, the same ripe smells of tobacco smoke, perfume, beer and piss.

By the time we get to Piccadilly Circus, I've had enough. The light here is blinding. The big screens flash daylight across streams of traffic and crowds. I stop, dazzled, with my head up, but the flow of people keeps going. They're drawn to the pulsing LEDs, advertising soft drinks and running shoes, like moths to a man-made moon. They jostle and push.

The power of artificial light is nothing new. In 1688, Louis XIV of France, Louis the Great, the Sun King, wanted to show his political and God-given might by illuminating Versailles with 24,000 candles. It was no doubt a fantastic sight, and probably uncommonly bright, but it is nothing to Piccadilly Circus, where lux readings have suggested that even at midnight the light is no dimmer than that of an overcast day.

The largest screen, only recently put in place, curves around the Regency architecture and up Shaftesbury Avenue. It is huge. Super bright. Super smooth. It screams modernity with each of its 11.6 million lights: easily outshining the Jumbotron installed only a couple of years before, its brilliance a message of never stopping, or at least never stop shopping. Switched on in 2017, plans are already in place to replace it. It is progress at the speed of light.

The brightness has not just grown but spread over and into the buildings. I can see now how the Regency architecture is hidden under a crust of artificial light. The old facades, which elsewhere are syrupped in street glare, have been completely hidden by light that crawls across its surface.

I'm not sure whether it's that I'm now footsore and weary, or just because of the lights, but the fun of Soho

has gone. For me Piccadilly Circus isn't just an advertise-
ment for the various trappings of modern life – Coke,
cars or clothes – but a symbol of how we've separated
the urban world from the natural one. Each flash, each
burning pixel, encapsulates the cry of Futurist Filippo
Tommaso Marinetti: 'Let's murder the moonlight!'

I feel dizzy with it all. And suddenly very tired. My
eyes are aching with the brightness. The noise and bustle. Two people are shouting at each other. They bawl
and push like rubbish human stags. A cyclist cuts across
traffic and a taxi driver slams on his horn. The noise is
quieter than the light.

After the giddy lights we both want somewhere softer,
calmer. We head towards Mayfair's red brick and stucco
columns, the crowds dwindling to nothing. The stillness
is a balm. We sit on a bench in Grosvenor Square and
gather ourselves. The light puddles on the pavement.
The sky itself is a dome of orange, as if all were on
fire; the clouds bright streaks of smoke. Despite the

approach of autumn the night is still mild. Urban areas can be up to 10°C warmer at night than the surrounding countryside: heat trapped by roads, pavements and buildings slowly released to join the heat from air vents and traffic.

I stare upwards, trying to see beyond the lights of London to the lights of the sky. I try to find Mars again, but the glare is too much. Perhaps it has set already, or maybe a whole planet has been lost to the creep of the horizon. The moon, last seen like a pale, nibbled communion wafer over St Paul's Cathedral, has dimmed further. A few stars, disconnected by light and cloud, are visible as the palest, fuzziest motes of light. Without the constellations, the guiding stars, I need an app to find my bearings.

I move my phone across the sky, the app on screen filling in the missing constellations, sheathed planets and hidden asterisms. A 'here's-what-you-could-have-won' of the night. The stars I can see with my naked eye are Deneb, the nineteenth brightest, the tail end of the Swan and the North Star: still offering direction to any lost Londoners who'd care to heed it.

We start to head south, towards Westminster, passing Claridge's, the Dorchester, where my great grandfather once worked, and the Hilton. The backs of the hotels are a hive of industry. Packages, parcels. Dented white vans with deep bins full of sheets and laundry. The labour for the luxury, the swan's feet swoosh of the swish hotel. The air is scented with fabric softener and diesel. Fag smoke and steam.

In the Hard Rock Cafe the cleaners are in, vacuuming and steaming. One man nods, surprised, as I raise a hand. While there are definitely fewer people around, especially here, it seems businesses are starting to limber up for the day ahead. The city's fracturing of the diurnal–nocturnal rhythm – its easing away from nature, like a ship from a dock – might have revolutionised play, but also work and, of course, sleep.

Before the advent of industrial work schedules and the spread of light, some historians have suggested that sleep was not condensed into a single block. Instead, as the darkness rose, people settled into a first sleep, rousing in the middle of the night to talk, tell stories, pray, have sex. A second sleep would follow, which lasted until

dawn. While Ekirch has unearthed more than 500 refer-
ences to segmented sleeping patterns – from diaries, court
records, medical books, diaries and literature – the idea
is one that is disputed. Nevertheless, it is true that how
we sleep has shifted over the centuries. Bedtime no longer
tends to coincide neatly with the cycles of day and night.
And many people (less than a quarter)[12] don't manage
the seven to nine hours' sleep adults are said to need.[13] In
our modern society we put less value on sleep: working
later, studying, looking after family, having fun. And some
people claim they simply don't need that much sleep.

Thomas Edison, a man who did so much to push back
the night, was also an opponent of sleep. He claimed, 'Put
an undeveloped human being into an environment where
there is artificial light, and he will improve.' Edison, like
his rival Nikola Tesla, was said to have worked for days
without retiring to his bed. In an 1889 interview with
Scientific American, Edison claimed he slept no more than
four hours a day and he expected his employees to keep
pace with him.

'At first,' Edison said, 'the boys had some difficulty
in keeping awake, and would go to sleep under stairways

and in corners. We employed watchers to bring them out, and in time they got used to it.'

Some still see lack of sleep as a badge of honour. When I was working in newspapers, pulling fourteen- and fifteen-hour shifts was a point of pride. Coffee and fag fuelled.

Pushing on, working deep into the night, can be hard going. Our bodies scream for rest. Shift workers who try to sleep during the day are fighting bodies that are responding to light. To flip night and day is to suffer from an almost permanent jet lag. Yet, more and more people seem to be doing it. According to the Trades Union Congress, the number of people working nights increased by 260,000 (9 per cent) in the five years from 2012 to 2017, with Britain's late-night workforce standing at 3.2 million. This means that one in eight people work nights.

Staying up all night, at least consistently, has a price. Studies at the Sleep Performance Research Centre at Washington State suggest that police who regularly work at night are more likely to be injured, while research by the Institute of Health & Work (IWH) published in the

Journal of Occupational & Environmental Medicine found that men and women, young and old, whether manual or non-manual workers, were more likely to be hurt working during the evening, night or early hours of the morning.[14]

One of my friends, a former night-bus driver and long-haul trucker, admitted he had fallen asleep once behind the wheel. He said it was a worryingly regular occurrence, with some drivers passing off sleep-related accidents by claiming a dog or cat had run out in front of them.

As well as the mistakes, mishaps, trips and falls that are more likely with groggy jet-lagged brains, the night shift is associated with other serious, long-term conditions: heightened risk of stroke and heart attack, links with cancer.[15] It can be harder to find time to exercise, to maintain a healthy diet. Research even suggests there is an impact on our bodies at a genetic level. By pushing back the night, we pay by bringing chaos to our biological processes.

Shift workers may bear the brunt of the night-time revolution, yet we are all affected by an increase in artificial light. Stuart Peirson, associate professor at

Oxford University and group leader in the Sleep and Neuroscience Institute, explained to me how street-lights, TVs, computer screens and home lighting can all help to create a disconnect between the systems whose synchronicity is believed to control our patterns of sleep.

The cues of light and darkness regulate our circa-dian clock. Artificial light in the evening throws off that natural rhythm, delaying sleep. And, put simply, not enough sleep can kill you. As Dr Peirson says, 'Animal studies have shown that if animals are sleep deprived for long periods then they die and it's typically due to infec-tion and sepsis. It causes the collapse of the immune function. At root it's probably long-term stress. We know long-term stress suppresses immune function. Certainly long-term sleep deprivation can be stressful. Even short-term studies of sleep have shown that if you deprive people of sleep for even one day they are stressed.'

I think of all those people I've seen working tonight, pushing against biological cues, influenced by artificial ones, and the risks they face of a weakened immune sys-tem. Our bodies, evolved from the gentle swing of day to night, cannot adapt to the speed of light. The city's freedom from nature comes at a cost.

It is nearly 3 a.m. when we reach Westminster Bridge. Big Ben trussed and wrapped like a leg of lamb. A bodge job of boards and poles. Only on the east side can you see the clock face. A moony eye that looks out on a river rashed with light. A few buses move past, blocks of lit air, purring to the kerb to let no one in and let no one off. But the pavements, guarded by elephant-grey humps of concrete and a girder security barrier, are empty.

The city is laid bare. Reduced to bones of concrete and glass. To lines of roads and light. To CCTV cameras that now have no one else to watch. I wonder if someone, somewhere, has been watching our bumbling nocturnal ambulation around the city. I wonder if they questioned what the hell we were doing.

I stand on the bridge next to Shaun and look down at the river, the water slashed and burned with red and orange light, baubles and pinpricks. The current churns and rips past buoys and the bridge pier in a flare of white. Downstream, apartments and office blocks cast oranges and purples into the water.

Some of the patches of light seem to come from the water itself: gleaming up like wraiths rising from the muddy depths.

There is an unsettling atmosphere to the night here. Shaun says he has never known London so still. I think of the witching hour. The time of night when all stops. It's a term that reminds me, without fail, of Roald Dahl's BFG, of my mum and dad reading it to me by the light of a bedside lamp.

There is certainly an unrealness to it all. A feeling of magic that I had, in all honesty, given up on finding in London. I wonder if it is the presence of Westminster's gas lights, the ragged twilight fringe of their glow that never quite extinguishes darkness. Yet, it is probably my imagination, romanticising the night again. There are enough electric lights close by to mean their presence is nothing more than aesthetic.

I think this feeling is more to do with the lack of people. The maddening pulse of the city, finally slowed and sleepy. But although I can feel my body is tired, my eyes and my feet sore, I'm also buzzing. I have a pill-popping, agitated energy, so unlike the times I have walked or sat in the natural night of the countryside. The wash of darkness, alleviated by the gentle lights of stars and the moon, soothes. Artificial lights feel as if they have burned into me, scorching senses, flicking too many switches in a sleep-deprived brain.

At points during the night I have enjoyed participating in the brightness, the madness. But I've spent too many hours trapped by London's light, over-whelmed by it. In the city it is so hard to escape it. Yet I'm surprised how much I feel it after just one night, as if it has taken a toll on me physically and emotionally.

Perhaps there's not much that can be done to reverse the illumination of our cities. It's not practical to suggest that we all relinquish our lights. But there are ways to control the level of illumination. The City of London is looking at replacing 15,000 streetlights, using LEDs to focus their output. A new control management system has also been put in place, allowing the authorities to adapt levels of lighting 'according to need', providing darker areas, including by the river.

Internationally too, cities have been working on the problems of artificial lighting. A Lights Out program has seen New York, Chicago and Houston, as well as major cities in Canada, turning off lights or dimming them for up to five months of the year in a bid to stop the glare that confuses migrating birds. Earth Hour sees public buildings and monuments around the globe turn off their lights in a sign of environmental solidarity. Campaigns to save energy, memorial events, anniversaries, including the centenary of Britain entering the First World War, also see lights being turned out.

But the chances to see natural light and natural night are brief and few. A dark night has become an attraction, a rarity, something to take notice of and marvel at, rather than something vital and natural, in the same way that festivals of light were once enjoyed in the pre-modern age.

Perhaps it is to be expected. Cities, places where there are people, will always be artificially lit. We have grown too used to electricity, too desensitised to its brightness, unaware of the biological and cultural cost. Yet in an age where we talk constantly of reconnecting people to nature, of creating green spaces in urban areas, of saving energy, it feels as if we should be able to create dark space too; places where the stars and the moon can be experienced without having to travel to the most remote corners of the country. Once we used technology to push back the night. Surely now we can use it to reclaim it, to revel in it, to live in it. Otherwise we run the risk that light will continue to spread, from cities, to towns and into the countryside. Night will be carved into an ever-thinner and increasingly dull strip.

5

Caught in the Light

The Christmas lights will soon be switched on in the centre of Bury St Edmunds. It seems to happen earlier each year. They are already strung across walkways, looped in shop windows and dangled from trees. Fairy lights, LEDs, incandescent bulbs that will strobe and pulse like the sides of deep-sea fish.

In a single Norwegian maple that stands between the Corn Exchange and the Nutshell, a pub already full to overflowing, a series of circular glass bands twist and turn in the breeze. Even without power, they sparkle and glitter as they move, candied glass that reflects the light cast from windows and streetlamps.

This tree is about to be decorated again. Half an hour after the autumn-weak sun finally sinks, the first bird arrives; shooting into upper branches that still cling to most of their leaves.

Another, then another. All perch on the same slim twig; nudging each other along, calling greetings and contact calls of *chizzick* and *swi-woo*. Move over. Move over.

I watch them, bobbing and swishing their tails up and down in a nervous, saucy fluttering. The pied wagtail really is a bird that lives up to its name. Its cheeks and belly moon-white, the rest of its body coloured in coal blacks and twilight greys.

They fidget and twitch. Little movers. Tiny dancers.

I can see from around the base of the tree, the lack of guano haloing its trunk, that the birds have not yet arrived in full force. I can see only about thirty. By later this month up to 500 wagtails will be roosting here, benefiting from safety in numbers and the retained heat that radiates from pavements, from shops and from light. Or perhaps they choose this maple for its decorations; each bulb a feather-warming three-bar fire.

London was so bright it feels as if its glow still coats me. I am phosphorescent. A Ready Brek man pumping out megawatts of stored light. I've walked around my hometown of Bury at night many times since that first snowy walk in the woods and I realise I've always avoided the light, seeking those places where it is darkest. I've haunted scraps of woodland, parks and river walks. Now I feel more aware of the light, I can't help but see more and more of it: to notice how it is spreading, creeping into the countryside.

Knowing how disruptive light can be to humans, I've been wondering what the impact is on the natural world: the blackbird singing under the lights in London; the wagtails in the town centre; the thousands on thousands of nocturnal and crepuscular species. Across the world a huge slice of our ecosystem is adapted to the conditions of natural night and natural light. Invertebrates, badgers, bats, the majority of smaller carnivores and rodents, 20 per cent of primates, 80 per cent of marsupials and many others are all night dwellers, night feeders, night breeders, night needers.

So tonight I don't want to hide from the light, but to notice it. I want to take another look at my hometown to see how far the light has spread, and think about how the nocturnal wildlife that lives in these habitats could be impacted by it. Is there anywhere in a modern, rural town where the night is not unnaturally bright?

While humans have chosen to walk into the light, dressed their world in it, these creatures have no such choice. As with so much else, they live with the consequences of our actions.

Several hours later I leave my friends in a town-centre bar and head east towards the outskirts where the lights stick to the roads. Apart from when the pubs, restaurants and clubs kick out, it's rare to see another human on foot round here after dark. The town at night empties. A complex social structure disappears with the sun, to leave a network of roads and paths, littered with fag ends, reflective crisp packets and the droopy skins of used condoms. It is a place patrolled by cats, some of which follow me for miles at a time, meowing forlornly as if all have forgotten them.

These areas belong to the local wildlife at night. But while the streets might be devoid of people, they're still full of their artificial lights.

The same is true across the country. Dark nights are on the wane. Just 21.7 per cent of England has pristine skies according to a survey by the Campaign to Protect Rural England. The highest levels of light come from towns and cities, major roads and airports, but light pollution spreads into the countryside too. Between 1992 and 2009 there has been a 39 per cent increase in dimly lit places across the UK and a 19 per cent increase in brightly lit areas.

The problem of artificial lighting is not confined to wealthy countries like the UK and the USA either – those places that are brightest on global maps of night – it is there too in the flares from oil wells along the African coast, in the squid lures and fishing-boat lights far out to sea. It is there in everyday, run-of-the-mill places like Bury St Edmunds.

I walk downhill then turn left, looping around the town centre until the shopping centre emerges on the left, lit with twinkling bands. The shoppers have gone but the lights are still on. The trunk road where I'm walking is always illuminated. All night. Every night. The cobra-heads of streetlamps hum with power, their heads holding shark-teeth rows of piercing LEDs.

Over the past decade, many of our streetlights have been replaced with these energy-efficient LEDs, but badly designed lights, no matter how modern, still leak light, and while LED lights are being used more frequently, in private homes as well as on the street, their efficiency and low cost might mean there are more lights overall.[16] Lights dimmed, or turned off at midnight by local authorities only looking to save money, will click on once more. And they can be incredibly bright, a daylight-strength light that many, including Bob Mizon, coordinator of the British Astronomical Association's Commission for Dark Skies, say is simply not needed at night.

I stop at the top of a new business estate that has been built on higher ground to the far east of the town, a place of grass bunds bristling with plastic-wrapped saplings and warehouses, which although empty are busy with light. I've seen wildlife up here earlier in the year, while the last building was being finished off. Skylarks sang over the snark of angle grinders biting into metal and hares raced over the rough grass between warehouse and road.

Tonight there is little obvious movement. I clamber up onto a bank and look west, back the way I've come. The divide between old and new lighting is clear to see. Around half of the town, the Victorian suburbs, the older estates, twinkles sodium orange, while the other half, wrapped in a shell spiral of brightly lit road, is white with LEDs. The clouded sky above the town buzzes with light. It reminds me of a pint of Guinness yet to settle.

My watch shows midnight and from where I stand I can see some of the lights, including around where I live, are clicking off. A wedge here, a clump there. I was expecting the impact to be more dramatic, the lessening of light to be greater, but the sky still burns.

It seems obvious that light levels like this must be having an impact on the natural world, on the habits of both plant and animal species. Plants are more sensitive to red light and are likely to be more affected by the orange glow of high-pressure sodium lamps, while LED lighting and the higher temperature blue light it generally emits can create serious problems for animals, disrupting the circadian clock and physiology of a wide range of species.

Some examples of light pollution's impact on wildlife are, of course, well known. TV has shown us the horror of turtle hatchlings crushed under car wheels and feet after being drawn to coastal lights rather than the reflection of the moon on the sea. Newspapers in the USA covered a story about a flock of grebes who splintered neck and wing in a lit car park their instincts told them was a lake.

But the impact of artificial light is not limited to these isolated cases, times when the bodies pile up in numbers that cannot be ignored. A recent study estimates that between 100 million and 1 billion birds are killed in the USA alone as a result of light pollution, with birds either colliding with lit buildings, to which certain species are attracted in the same way a moth is drawn to a lamp, or becoming 'entrapped' and dying of exhaustion.[17] Another American study revealed that the number of migrating birds increases the closer you get to a city.[18]

In a related article in *Science Daily* it was claimed the effect of streetlights and the glare from buildings stretched for about 125 miles beyond any urban centre in the north-eastern United States, meaning there is no place in that region where the birds 'can't see the sky glow of a city'.

Birds are affected in other ways too, with circadian rhythms and breeding patterns all bending with the light. A study by scientists at the Max Planck Institute for Ornithology, published in 2015, suggested that birds singing at night – mostly blackbirds or robins, traditional early risers – were singing both later and earlier. Blackbirds living around artificial light produced young a whole month earlier.

In 2019, the British Trust for Ornithology launched a national survey of tawny owls after the bird – a species whose call evokes night – slipped onto the Amber List of Birds of Conservation Concern. It is thought that increasing urbanisation and light pollution could be impacting on their populations.

The more we look, the more damage light pollution seems to do, its impact far-ranging, running up and
down the food chain, changing the time flowers bloom,
how beetles navigate and hunt. While the bright lights
of humans create biological chaos for us, the same is
true for wildlife. Light and the retreat of night doesn't
just impact on single species in isolation, but on whole
ecosystems.

Catherine Rich and Travis Longcore, writing in the
introduction to their groundbreaking book of scientific
papers, *Ecological Consequences of Artificial Night Lighting*,
put it well. 'What,' they said, 'if we woke up one morning only to realise that all of the conservation planning
of the last thirty years told only half the story – the
daytime story? Our diurnal bias has allowed us to ignore
the obvious, that the world is different at night and that
natural patterns of darkness are as important as the light
of day to the functioning ecosystems.'

It was their research, and the integration of the find-
ings of international studies, that took the issue of light
pollution beyond the human. In fact, 'light pollution'
itself was a term they quickly discarded: too focused

on the sky, too concerned with human interactions with the astronomical. After all, even lights shining the right way, i.e. downwards, can impact on animals. Instead, they wrote of artificial night lighting: light generated by human activity that bleeds into and corrodes the natural patterns of light and dark.

Their book is eye-opening. Each section addresses the effects of artificial night lighting on different taxonomic groups: mammals, birds, reptiles, amphibians, fish, invertebrates and plants. The narrative though, no matter what the species, runs along familiar and worrying lines: artificial lighting disrupts foraging patterns and increases risk of predation.

Travis also told me about new research he was doing, in which he is attempting to show how animals see the landscape. By taking photographs and then increasing the exposure, he creates an image that represents what creatures capable of seeing in low light experience. He showed me a couple on his laptop that were taken while looking out from the Hollywood Hills. The first showed a dark landscape, with a view over a sea of lights. The second image, enhanced in line with the visual capabilities of a mountain lion, was a glimpse of a bright, new world. The city was no longer a bright twinkling, but an impenetrable, blazing wall. The mountain, the trail, both invisible in the first image, were lit up as if it were day.

What is dark to our eyes today, what feels natural, is quite simply not. There are biological factors at play, the fact that without a tapetum lucidum to capture more light, with fewer rods in our eyes than many nocturnal species, the world at night is darker for us. But it is cultural too. We have become unused to the darkness, to the subtleties of natural light. Cocooned in electric brightness, even nights where the moon and stars are bright seem, at least at first glance, coal-hole black.

Travis said that light levels recorded at the spot where the photograph was taken were always brighter than that cast by the full moon. Without the seasonal cycle of wax and wane, the natural cycles of light and dark are disrupted and the circadian clock becomes confused. As a result, navigation and spatial awareness in animals is disturbed. Trees and plants are affected too, holding on to their leaves or prematurely bursting into bud.

A European Research Council-funded project called Ecolight has been studying just these effects. Much of its work has involved looking at grass verges, and with good reason. The hundreds of thousands of miles of roads that crisscross the UK contain a significant percentage of our natural and semi-natural grassland; equal to at least half of that found within increasingly rare flower-rich grasslands and meadows. As a result, most of our wildlife is a few metres away from the road or on the outskirts of towns and villages. Verges are lifelines. And they are well lit.

Dr Jonathan Bennie, a lecturer in physical geography at the University of Exeter, explained that Ecolight set up field experiments, trying to see what happened when they exposed simple plots, designed to mimic habitats found in verges, to light. Some plots contained just plants, while others were populated with herbivores and predators – beetles, ladybirds, aphids and slugs – to try to separate out how the effects of light might cascade through the food chain.

The results were both clear and complex. Light changed the behaviour of both flora and fauna, but the implications travelled both from the top of the food chain to the bottom and from the bottom to the top. Plants were seen to behave in a way that affected their aphid populations, something that had knock-on effects up the food chain, while the foraging patterns of ground beetles were also altered, increasing slug numbers and thereby having impacts at the base of the food chain.

Perhaps what was surprising, though, was not that light, the lessening of night's natural dark, had caused changes – but how much it had changed *everything* in often unpredictable ways. Shine a light on a species and you will be able to record a reaction, a difference in growth or population dynamic. But unpicking the outcome of that reaction for a whole ecosystem growing into a new, brighter world is much more difficult.

While some nocturnal species seemed to stop hunting in the night, others increased, picking off their prey with ever-greater efficiency. Diurnal species of spider and beetle also became more active, creating knock-on effects for their prey animals. There were also physiological effects, including the disruption of reproductive cycles. And while light caused disorientation, it also became a trap.

I know exactly how these creatures must feel. Even though the brightness here is nothing compared with London, where at least the streets were lit for *someone*, I am surprised at how much artificial light there is once you start looking for it.

The solution seems simple. Introduce legislation to ensure that light is appropriate for its location and switched off, or simply not installed, when it is not needed. Currently there are guidelines but no set laws regarding the use of lighting, even in many areas that are designated as National Parks or Areas of Outstanding Natural Beauty.

The CPRE, the countryside charity – an organisation with a history of campaigning to protect and improve dark skies – has certainly pushed for change. In May 2018, it asked for a stiffening of wording around light pollution, including around the lighting of existing developments. While it wants to see lit areas become less bright, it also asked for the government to pay closer attention to 'relative darkness' to prevent the slow creep of light's trespass.

The ask seems modest and entirely reasonable – something that would improve human health, protect wildlife and help reconnect us to the landscape and starscape of night. But concerns over safety and crime, despite research suggesting the turning off of lights does not impact negatively on either,[19] have so far proved a barrier to progress.

The clouds over the town, glowing the colour of a newt's belly, bring drizzle. A half-hearted rain in a half-hearted dark. I keep walking, following the road. Over traffic lights, clicking through changes for no one but themselves, and over roundabouts. I've driven this route and walked it in the daytime countless times, but at night with the streets empty, there is a real sense of being led by infrastructure: by the slip, slap of foot on slab and kerb, but also by the pull of light. The route is marked out and must be followed. I find the lack of choice irritating, monotonous, prescriptive.

When the chance comes to step away from the road I take it, peeling off down a path that leads round Holywater Meadows. Deep into the winter this route becomes almost impassable as the water finds its old home, the tributaries of the Lark swelling and wallowing out onto the land. But now it is still relatively dry and screened by scrub well on its way to becoming wet woodland; it is also relatively dark. The night has been snagged on hawthorn and entwined in elder.

Even though I have been out for hours, I have been almost constantly under lights and my eyes have not adjusted to darkness. I must listen instead. I stop and cup my ears. There the River Linnet sogging along, percolating through leaf drip and litter, there the *rip-chew* of sheep still grazing, and in among the understorey the *zip-crack* of movement. Scurrying and hurried. Mouse? Vole? Rat?

I try to walk behind what lights there are, stalking the verges, wading in hedges full of things thrown from cars: bottles of piss in unhealthy shades, sandwich boxes, carrier bags. But it feels as though the light is coming from everywhere, casting down from clouds, glaring up from puddled water and wet road. Even more comes from the Greene King Brewery to my left: the building's lights reflecting off a pile of steel barrels three storeys high.

A Donkey Kong ammunition stash that blushes Jaffa orange.

I can't help but feel snared by the lights I walk through. A muntjac, hidden in scrub, bolts as I get too close, its back flashing orange from the brightness that surrounds the roadside. At night it is easy to see how those green and darker places where wildlife can get a foothold are broken up by glare and glow. Habitat is cut by lights.

Part of it is the roads. As I head further out of town, it feels as if this isn't a place for any living thing; it is a route for cars, for speed and aggression. It's by no means unusual to see large numbers of dead animals around here. They lie, scattered, broken and twisted, on hard shoulders and against the central reservation. Among car parts and litter are the bodies of deer – muntjac, fallow and red – foxes, badgers, rabbits, hedgehogs and the occasional too-curious cat.

Although it seems logical to think that bright lights make animals more visible to drivers and therefore less likely to be hit, there is really nothing to back it up. A study in the USA suggested that increased lighting on highways was not effective at cutting down the number of deer–vehicle collisions.[20] In fact, they could even make things worse.

Emerging from the relative darkness of the surrounding area into a light-soaked environment overwhelms nocturnal animals' night vision. For a few precious moments they are effectively rooted to the spot. Blind and terrified. It reminds me of a passage from *Watership Down*, of going 'tharn' in the light. While looking at the flattened corpse of a hedgehog, Bigwig explains how 'at night the hrududil have great lights, greater than Frith himself. They draw creatures toward them, and if they shine on you, you can't see or think which way to go. Then the hrududu is quite likely to crush you.'[21]

The modern nightscape of bright roads, light-leaking homes and streetlights, whose glare trespasses and bleeds almost everywhere, disrupts and confuses how and where animals move, or prevents navigation altogether.

Even creatures that fly are reluctant to cross lit areas. Bats are true creatures of the night: they are made of it. Shadows made solid. They navigate the world with both powerful night vision and echolocation, flipping between the two as needed. In low light levels they can effectively switch off the stream of pips and squeaks that help create a sound map of the night to conserve energy and sneak up on the species of moths whose sensitive ears are tuned into their hunting techniques.

For bats, like deer and other nocturnal animals, entering an area of artificial light is similar to us staring into the sun. The glare, or even the reflected glare, can cause them to miss objects: to collide and die.

Some bigger, slower-flying types of bats, such as brown long-eared, greater horseshoe and Natterer's bats, used to operating in complete darkness very late at night to avoid avian predators, are particularly affected by light. They now occupy a world where they are often visible and, as a result, more vulnerable.

Of course, there may be winners too, animals that have adapted to the new, artificially light skies. Fast-flying pipistrelle bats can treat lights, which trap moths and flying insects, as bug buffets. Yet even this offers only a short-term competitive advantage. The light creates an unbalancing of the prey–predator relationship and has implications for future invertebrate populations.

Or, to put it another way, how much future bat food is available.

And that will also have a knock-on effect as the consequences of light cascade and build, disturbing entire ecosystems across different habitats.

As I walk, I think about the network of roads visible from the estate above Bury. It is a tangle of light, the landscape a maze for any creature that depends on darkness. While we think of our illuminations as creating safety, for much of our nocturnal wildlife we have constructed an intricate, glowing network of barriers. As Dr Bennie said, the nightscape has become a 'fearscape'.

I decide to head back to the river in the hope of finding some wildlife on its banks, walking towards the cathedral that stands orange on the horizon and the corridors of green that crisscross the town. The rain has started again and I feel grumpy about being forced to walk on concrete. I want grass and mud and dark.

By the football ground at Rams Meadow the Lark has fought its way through weir and flood defence to get here and the energy has gone out of it. It struggles for breath and barely moves. Puddles. Congealed and black under willow and alder. I pad along the riverside path and listen to a few birds moving about in the cover, resettling in the light-dappled canopy.

A drizzling mist hangs in the river's shallow valley, stretching along its length. A ghost of a flow, a reminder of the river's presence in a town that hardly notices its existence. But I feel happier, less exposed, now that I'm off the road and into the shade of trees.

As my mood improves, I notice I'm talking to myself. It's not the first time. I've often found that I'm jabbering away, almost unconsciously, when I walk at night. I reason with myself, encourage, chide and ask questions:

Are you all right?

Where shall we go now?

Why don't we go home?

Sometimes I hum. A responsibility-free David Cameron kind of tune. *Do-dooooo-doo-do*.

The brain resigned to no company but itself.

It has been an eye-opening night. One that has made me think about the landscape I live in, but also about some of the work I have been involved in. For the last five or six years I have worked with the Wildlife Trusts, promoting a vision of a 'wilder' Suffolk. It is about not just limiting nature to the pockets of reserves under the Trusts' protection but encouraging wildness to spread through the countryside: across sustainable farmland, along hedgerows, rivers, wood, parks and verge.

Until now I have never really thought about how a lack of natural darkness can be a problem too. I can't help but feel worried that, however good our intentions, conservation can do only so much while night is chased away.

Environmental news has certainly made for grim reading over the past few years. Die-offs. Extinction. The collapse of invertebrate populations. Invariably, whether in thought pieces or discussions, someone will mention how we no longer find our home windows or headlights covered with insects. I wonder if it is an example, not just of the rate of decline, but the cause: that light is part of the same toxic cocktail as habitat fragmentation and human development. By chasing away darkness and hiding the cues given by natural light we have created another imbalance in the natural world that impacts on plants, pollinators, mammals, birds and, eventually, us.

Across the road, the river flows again, into and under the car park of the supermarket that is still very much open. Twenty-four hours of shopping, twenty-four hours of light. Jen has asked me to pick up some milk and cereal for the kids' breakfasts, 'to make myself useful while I'm wandering around like an idiot' but I can't face going in yet. The lights are too intense after the sliver of dark that I have been following. Their glare feels like a clear demarcation of where the natural world stops and the human one begins, and it is clear how much the latter is encroaching on the former.

Things can change, they must. But it will take legislation from a responsible government to encourage local authorities, responsible for most of the UK's streetlights, to dim or turn off the lights for reasons other than cost – to make sure that the blight of artificial light does not continue to spread. As individuals we have a role to play too. Not only do we need to be ethical consumers, thoughtful light installers, but we actually need to step outside. By seeking darkness and the natural lights of the night, to acclimatise to it, to watch and notice the changes of the moon, the seasonal wheeling of the stars, we will know what we are saving and what could be lost.

I look at the roundabout hunched in the road, thick with woods, an embankment rising up to meet the A14 flyover, before sloping down again towards the road to the sugar-beet factory. I wait for a small flurry of traffic – a lorry, a taxi and an ambulance with blues and twos – and jog cross the main road.

The undergrowth is thick, wetting me up to my knees. I ease through the trees, young beech and birch, and into a clearing. I've always found there's something fascinating about roundabouts. I think it probably stems from a J. G. Ballard book, *Concrete Island*, about an architect who crashes through a safety barrier to become marooned: unable to climb the embankment or flag down a passing car. They are dead spaces. Ignored. A bit like the suburban night. Ripe for exploration.

I sit on a hubcap, frisbied in off a passing car, and pour tea from my Thermos. I open my packet of biscuits, happy with myself. Free in the night.

Do-dooooo-doo-do.

The rain has eased but water still drips from the canopy that almost shuts out the light-stained clouds. The birches have been shedding branches and the eyes on their trunks are black against the milk-white of their papery bark.

A car moves around the roundabout, its headlights arcing in through the trees, its wheels shushing through the standing water on the road. The little woodland recovers its darkness and silence.

Then among the splats of water dripping from the trees comes a call. A tawny *ke-wick*. Loud, almost directly above me; its call echoing over leaf, rotten wood, plastic bags and car parts.

Ke-wick.

Ke-wick.

The voice of the night.

A female, alone and unanswered.

I'm delighted to have company. I look for her, but she is too well hidden, too camouflaged, seeking out her own patch of darkness. I wonder if she sees me, I wonder what she sees.

I finish my tea, pack my bag and stand up. It's time to go shopping. The clouds have finally cleared and the sky, with less to reflect the town's light, is a dark aubergine, dotted with a few smashed-glass stars. I can see the horns of Aries, the fish of Pisces hung out to smoke in the steam of the sugar-beet factory.

A police car slows, makes a circuit of the roundabout and then pulls into the car park.

I jog across the road and head for the shop entrance. The police car's window comes down and an officer leans out. He wants to know what I'm doing.

I wave a half-eaten biscuit at him, still walking.

'Having a cup of tea with an owl.'

6

Living in the Dark

Light forms into long crystals on the ceiling. Jagged peaks and steep cliffs. Ice white. Fluted and fluttering with the movements of the curtains that don't quite fit.

The room is quiet. The sound of deep sleep.

I get up and tiptoe to the window, watching the pattern of light change as headlights sweep along the road three storeys down. Out to sea, in the Sound of Mull, there are buoys flashing. Winking out of time. Red, red, green, signalling rock and reef.

Inland, the lights of Oban are still on. The bay is an arc of light. Lanterns swagged from shops, bars and restaurants. On Battery Hill, the high crag overlooking the town, the miniature colosseum of McGaig's tower glows a Cadbury-wrapper purple.

I'd walked through the town earlier with my daughter Eliza, eating in a restaurant that looked out over the water. Seth, feeling unwell from eight and a half hours penned in a car, had gone back to the hotel with Jen.

Eliza was excited that we were alone, eating out in 'a proper grown-up restaurant'. I fed her bits of my crab while she hoovered up pizza and talked at a million miles an hour. We chatted about school, about friends, about jobs and getting a dog.

I wanted to know what she thought about the lights that formed colourful slicks on the water's surface and fizzed from shopfronts. For her they were pretty, they added something. The idea of having no lights seemed completely alien. Almost inhuman. Born into the dark of winter, a solstice, snow baby, she has grown up surrounded by light. Why, she asked, would I want 'everything so dull'?

In just two hours, it will be time to get up to catch the ferry out to the Isle of Coll. Designated a Dark Sky Community by the International Dark Sky Association in

2013, there is not a single streetlight across its 30 square miles. Past the Sound of Mull, it is a scrap of wave-lashed land where nights remain deep and dark. The stars and the moon, the shades of natural light are still sacred.

After realising just how much light pollution there is across the UK, even where I live, I wanted to come here to experience one of these Dark Sky Communities. Part of me, of course, wants to experience what it's like to walk under a sky that is entirely clear of artificial light, to navigate using only the natural light of the night. But also, I want my children to experience it, to change their expectations of what night is and what it can be.

I've been looking forward to this trip. Even with the ever-present lights of town, I've been watching the skies change as the clocks go back. The stars ticking towards the change of the season. The hours tilting with the earth. The night rushing in, the dark rising.

Our apartment, when we reach it, like all homes on Coll, has been left unlocked. We are staying in the island's capital of Arinagour, a small cluster of a low white houses, a post office, shop, community centre and hotel, which forms a barnacle crust on the south side of Loch Eatharna. Our windows overlook the calm water of the bay and the old pier: its flat, wet cobbles sticking out like a fat, grey tongue.

We spend most of the day unpacking and recovering from the early start. The kids are narked and irritable. They bicker and fight, baulking at my suggestion to play outside; pointing at the fizzing bands of rain blowing in off the sea.

The seals are the only things that seem to stop the squabbles. We take it in turn to use binoculars and watch their heads pop above the waves, before they sink slowly back down, noses pointing up, as if extracting them-selves from a tight sweater.

Jen is curled up on the sofa in front of a freshly set fire and part of me desperately wants to join her. She has declared this a day of soup and red wine, jumpers and duvets.

'You can walk if you want,' she says, 'but I'm not budging.'

So I leave the apartment alone as the moon begins to rise, its light bleaching the horizon to the north-east, and follow the single-lane road that hugs the edge of the bay. The only light I can see comes from two windows of the hotel. A hand-painted sign, dancing with the wind on the wire fence, says 'To the church'. I follow it up a steep shingle track.

From the foot of the bay the church looks imposing. A sentinel on its rock, looming over Arinagour since 1907. But up close and in the darkness the church is small, cosy-looking. Even the gravestones seem to huddle up to its walls. The window of the bell tower is covered with a red wooden shutter that matches the colour of the door and window frames. There is no stained glass here. I wonder if the plainness is due to expense or some historically held spartan view. Perhaps there was simply no need to paint pictures of heaven onto glass when it streams through the windows every night.

As well as still being a place of worship, this church is one of Coll's three Dark Sky Discovery Sites, a place where the sightlines are uninterrupted. The stars join up the horizons, from north to south, east to west.

The UK Dark Sky Discovery partnership, a network of national and local astronomy and environmental organisations led by the Science and Technology Facilities Council, was set up in 2011. Its aim was simply to make it easier for people to engage with astronomy and the night sky.

The Discovery Sites are separate from the Dark Sky designations bestowed by the IDA, but they are meant to complement them. After all, even when landscapes are lauded for their lack of light pollution, there can be confusion about where to go for the best viewing points.

Importantly these sites aren't located just where the darkness is as deep as Coll. Since the project's launch in 2011 there are now more than 150 Discovery Sites across the UK, from remote rural spots to parks in more urban areas, from Cornwall to Caithness. After all, while the likes of Galloway and Coll are spectacular, they are not particularly easy to get to, especially if you live among the bright lights of lowland England. Many Discovery Sites are found in more accessible locations and are suitable for both expert stargazers and those venturing out for the first time. They are divided into two categories:

Milky Way sites, where the arm of our galaxy, with its hard frost of stars, can be seen with the naked eye, and Orion sites, where the seven stars that form the famous winter hunter are visible.

All of Coll's are Milky Way sites, the darkest designation, and this one requires the shortest and easiest of walks (if you rule out the eight hours in a car and three hours on a ferry to reach the island). I leave the unfenced churchyard and scramble up a knoll, where granite pushes through sheep-nibbled grass. The wind threatens to topple me, whistling through gapped teeth, and causes a tarpaulin on a half-built house to snicker and flap like a land-locked sail.

Apart from the wind, though, all is quiet. I'm struck by the simplicity of it all. This little island seems bigger now, stretching out far beyond the waves of the sea loch that have been mercury-tipped by the moon. Form and boundaries have disappeared with the day.

The village too has relaxed into the night. The streets smoothed, the potholes filled, the wire of the fences rolled up and rubbed out. I think how I felt in the city, in the town: how streetlights brought tension, pushing the darkness away to rankle and complain in unsavoury alleys. But here, night unfolds gently. A cat yawn, stretching from coast to coast. It is embracing and comforting.

Above the church I can see the first stars beginning to appear, bright through scuds of pithy cloud. Vega, with it the lowered flag of Lyra, a harp dripping notes of light. The Northern Cross that forms the skeleton of Cygnus, her long neck craning across the sky; stretched out in flight and taut. There too is Polaris, Hercules and Mars: a hot coal cooling in the night. Many of the stars feel familiar now. Old friends to reach for and touch.

As twilight spreads, like ink on a wet page, the constellations and asterisms become harder to pick out among all the other stars. Stars, thousands of light years apart, have exploded into a glittering infinity, taking with them my rookie map of the night. I am disorientated. I stare hard at a patch of the sky I don't recognise for five minutes, cursing that I haven't brought my chart with me, before I realise it is the loping wingspan of Cassiopeia, queen of the night, freckled and smudged with stars usually veiled by light pollution.

I lie back on the rock, cushioned by the thickness of a coat that I struggled to pull on over layers of T-shirts and jumpers. My movement is so limited in all my clothes I wonder if I'll be able to get up. I am a turtle staring at the desert sun. I pull away my snood so I can breathe in the cold, imagining the darkness entering my lungs like smoke.

A headrush follows as my brain tries to process distance and size, depth and movement. I can feel each breath, each knock of my heart. The world swings. But now, I swing with it. I've learned to go with the feeling. Stargazing reminds me of horse riding, of letting your body sway with something bigger and stronger.

Don't resist, don't fight it, feel the motion.

The creep of cloud, pushed by wind, adds more movement, the dark shapes like the hulls of boats pushing through a luminescent sea. In their wake, the stars appear to spin across the sky. Harder. Faster.

A meteor shoots from Cygnus' rump to burn out by Cassiopeia's bright beak and then, like the shutters of the church, the night closes. The clouds collide and merge, scrubbing away the texture of the sky, leaving only the beluga-pale moon. A white ball in a pocket, snookered by cloud. I raise my binoculars for a last glimpse before it disappears. The angle of the sun in relation to the moon means the shadows on its surface are now clear: the acne scar of craters on its shoulder. The darkness of its howling maw. As I'm watching the detail begins to fade, until all is hidden behind a soft lowered lid of cloud.

The rain comes almost instantly.

There are a handful of people in the Coll Hotel when I go in dripping. They nod and carry on talking. Most are gathered at the chipped wooden bar, sitting on stools or standing with pints raised within striking distance of their lips. The barman explains that they've retreated from the lounge where the change in wind direction means the old coal fire is no longer drawing and the room, covered in maps and black and white photos, has filled with heavy smoke.

The conversation revolves around the ferry. Will it run, will it not? They are, and I admit I'm surprised, inclusive and welcoming. I was expecting the accents here to have that Hebridean lilt, a hint of Welsh or Irish that comes from the Gaelic influence, but it seems many are incomers. Some have links to the islands, relatives who have lived here for generations, whose homes passed down the family line, while others have been drawn by the memory of holidays. Pushed by noise. Pulled by quiet.

Kip, an artist who moved to Coll from Shropshire, tells me that now is a good time to visit. After a summer where the sun shines for up to twenty-two hours, with many of those filled with work, the island is ready to embrace winter, to change pace. The long nights, Kip says, mean a slowing down for all of the industries that rely on land and sea. The fishing boats do not go out at night. The coast, littered with wrecks – steamers, paddlers that have been 'star-blinded' by storms – is just too dangerous.

Darkness here is simply part of the everyday. Everyone is passionate about the life they have carved out on this Hebridean rock. For them, the dark skies seem to represent much more than a lack of light pollution (or a way of attracting tourists) – they are a chance to return to a more natural way of living, their daily activities influenced by the rising and setting of the sun.

The pints appear and disappear, the drinkers ducking in and out. Kip talks about the island, how Coll's produce is not labelled organic as everyone knows that no artificial fertilisers are used here. Kelp, washed up like tiny gelatinous palms, is ploughed into the earth. It is a place of essentials. Blood and bone. The darkness is part of that; it is a basic, fundamental thing. As fiercely guarded as any stone monument.

I ask if any newcomers ever try and introduce light to the island. A mutter ripples through the drinkers. Kip grins.

'There was one, who brought some very Glasgow ideas here. He wanted lights and speed bumps.'

Keith, listening to football on a radio channel that crackles through the TV, interrupts. 'Why do we need speed bumps when we've got sheep?'

Kip carries on. 'Yeah. Well, anyway . . . he died.' He motions to the landlord with his eyes to get a refill before continuing.

'But we had nothing to do with that.'

But he's also keen to point out that Coll is in no way backward. 'I guess you could say, we want the convenience of the modern world but none of the shit that goes with it.'

Certainly, there have been changes on Coll and some surprising heroes. In the hotel, Amazon is revered. Before it began its deliveries only two catalogues would send packages to the island and these were expensive. Returning anything was prohibitive. As a result, most of the men in the village all had the same trousers and the same shoes.

I laugh, thinking he's taking the piss.

'I'm serious.'

As the hours pass, various people enthusiastically suggest different spots for me to walk. Maps are drawn on the barman's receipt pad or scribbled in my notebook – the Gaelic names patiently spelled out. But most just tell me to look up.

'There's no light to bother you here.'

By the time I leave the bar, I'm fogged with drink, but the clouds have partly cleared. The stars form a breathy mist of smashed glass; the clouds that remain shine in the moonlight like old, burnished mirrors.

The sheep have come into the village when I leave the apartment in the morning. A woollen tide rubbing up against parked cars and standing around in gardens. I head east, looking over a sun-scalded sea towards Mull, Staffa, Treshnish, the sky clear but for a few dusty scraps of cloud. I'm glad the rain has broken but still not used to the cold blade of the wind.

Paula Smalley's B&B, Tigh na Mara, sits overlooking the bay on a high outcrop, before the road slopes back down to the new pier. It was Paula, together with Julie Oliphant, the owner of the Coll Hotel, and local stargazers Tony Oliver and Olvin Smith, who led the campaign to get recognition for the island's star-filled skies.

It all began with a conversation at the same bar I was at last night. The island of Sark in the Channel Islands had just been designated an International Dark Sky Community and the media was full of talk of Sark's lack of artificial lights. No streetlamps, no cars. Although Coll does have vehicles, the low population means it doesn't have the infrastructure, the shops, businesses and number of people demanding different things that make going 'light-free' in town such a challenge. There was a feeling that Coll could follow in Sark's footsteps both to protect the night skies and also, in a place that relies on tourism, to make it pay.

Although the gang of four led the charge, the whole island came together. Farmers were initially concerned that it could affect how they worked in the winter months, others worried that it would complicate development and planning – crucial for somewhere that is desperate to keep its young folk. But Paula says that once people realised they were not pushing for an end to light, but rather bad lights, the community was extremely supportive. Coll's children, who Paula says have 'grown up with the dark' and therefore don't fear it, were particularly involved.

The official announcement in 2013 was celebrated by everyone. More and more people – people like me, seeking natural darkness and natural light – now come to the island in winter.

I can't imagine there ever being a consensus in my own town, or many others to be honest, for lights to be dimmed or turned off. The introduction of a midnight switch-off in some areas to save energy and cut costs was controversial enough, provoking more furious letters to local newspapers than potholes or bin collections. But that's not to say we should give up on the idea.

Just as in the movement against climate breakdown, individual actions matter. Installing dimmers in your home and turning lights off can stop light seeping from houses, as well as save energy. If outdoor spaces need to be lit, fixtures can be used to minimise glare. The right type of bulb is also important. Bob Mizon, the UK coordinator for the Campaign for Darker Skies explained that Northumberland's Longstone Lighthouse – Britain's most powerful lighthouse – uses a 1,000W light source, but people are using 500W lights to illuminate even small back gardens.

We can lobby against harmful artificial light too. Write to councillors, MPs and demand change; petition for a law that will make fly-tipping light a crime in the same way as dumping rubbish is on land.

The benefits are clear, both for humans and the rest of the natural world. Paula suggests the campaign to protect Coll's darkness has certainly had positives beyond tourism. It has forced them to look up, to acknowledge that what they have got now is unusual; is precious.

'I remember when I was younger and my granddad was always keen on showing us the stars. But he said I was a lost cause. I just didn't get it. But since becoming involved with this group and being given the designation we have all learned so much.'

Paula, who has lived on Coll for twenty-five years, says there has also been a strengthening of the connection with the seasons over recent years. The dark winters that hold the island are as comforting as the spring bloom of the machair – a dune grassland unique to west Scotland and the north-west of Ireland – or the sight of basking sharks and otters.

I walk back to the apartment slowly, lingering by the rocks to watch the seals. The air is fresh with the sea.

It feels as if there is more oxygen than anyone could hope to breathe. Both Paula and the guys in the bar had mentioned how one of the things that was really special about the island is the chance to see the aurora borealis. The dark nights in the high latitudes of Coll mean that, although their displays are still few and far between, the Northern Lights do appear; the atmosphere lighting up gusts of charged solar particles in dancing waves of green, white and pink.

I know the chances of seeing them are slim, but they are not the only strange and beautiful thing that has the power to transform the night with natural light. Recently, I've been reading up on something called 'the night sun', a phenomenon that sees the sky lit by broad and intense luminous patches.

Recorded for centuries across the world in different countries and latitudes, these bright nights have largely disappeared with the spread of artificial light. Perhaps the most recent was observed in 2001 at the Leoncito Astronomical Complex, an observatory in the San Juan Province of Argentina, high in the Andes. Rebecca Boyle, writing in the *New Scientist*, says that during this event,

Steven Smith of Boston University in Massachusetts reported a night sky that was ten times lighter than would usually have been expected.

It is only recently that science has been able to explain what causes this phenomenon and pinpoint its increasing rarity. During the 1980s, Gordon Shepherd of York University in Toronto, Canada, built a satellite to monitor waves of air as they moved through the atmosphere. As well as noticing how the waves could pile on top of one another to produce columns of pressurised air, Shepherd also noticed how the chemical make-up of the light changed throughout the day. As Boyle puts it, 'During daylight hours, ultraviolet radiation from the sun splits molecular oxygen into individual atoms. When the sun goes down, the atoms rejoin. This produces a small amount of light, called airglow.'

Between 1991 and 2004 Shepherd realised airglow emissions varied, often in extremes, from night to night. Then, within the last few years, he made the connection between the atmospheric waves and the airglow; how the piled-up waves created a higher concentration of oxygen and a correspondingly higher glow. Following further research with colleague Young-Min Cho, an algorithm was produced that could trawl through their collected data, discarding nights where the brightness was caused by other factors such as the aurora. Their study showed that there was around twenty-five bright nights a year, but they happened in places where light pollution rendered them invisible.

I mull over something Paula kept saying: 'Without darkness, there is no light.' I think she meant it philosophically, a metaphysical point about how we view the darkness of night. But it is true practically as well. When the sky is naturally dark, other lights are revealed, some of which – like the night sun – we didn't even know we were missing out on. With too much artificial light there is a darkness of a different kind in our lives.

The rain has been on and off all day but by evening it seems to have stopped for good. I drive west across the island, heading towards Calgary Point, where the land has been nibbled like an apple to the core, leaving rock and two sweeping beaches. The sun colanders through twists of wire-wool clouds, not drying the land but softening it. To the south I can see the highest peak of Mull, Ben More, cresting between chilly paps of rock. Its north side is snow-covered and barely there against a cuticle-pale sky, yet to be darkened by twilight.

Turbines spin so fast they look as if they could take off and the water of Loch na Cloiche and Loch Ronard rushes with the wind. Sharp wavelets burst white on to thin, brittle-looking peat banks.

I pull over a cattle grid and into the RSPB car park that is also the end of the public road. This is Totronald, one of the other sites that Paula suggested I visit. A place where even the official from the Dark Skies Association had been dazzled by the brightness of the stars. With the moon rising slightly later tonight I'm hoping to have a good viewing window. A sweet spot of deep darkness.

The last of the sunlight slants onto the machair. In spring and summer this landscape is awash with colour, humming with insects, rasping with corncrake. But now, lit by weak sunlight that turns it the colour of weathered copper, it has its own bleak beauty. In all my visits to the

Hebrides I've never seen it in bloom. For me, machair is a word like tundra – evocative of north, of cold and of dark.

While the corncrake might have left weeks ago to winter in Africa, the geese are here. White-fronted and barnacle. Greylags as big as dogs. They graze on the machair, bark at every unexpected footstep and leave turds like giant green Wotsits curled on almost every track and path.

I walk as the light falls, the signs of night not only in the sky, but in the increasing whiteness of the rocks. They glow like cheap solar lamps in a landscape that is smoothed and rounded by the gathering dark. I find it hard to make out the path. The footworn grass disintegrates into sheep runs, cow paths and the traces of quad-bike tracks. Even after last night I'm surprised at how quickly night rises this far north. The twilights seem to overlap like breaking waves, with astronomical twilight, true dusk, arriving only an hour or so after the sun sets.

The light disappears in a gasp. But returns just as quickly. It is as if a switch has been flicked, or an unseen, silent generator has kicked into life. Mars, hanging red and lonely, is joined by a mass of stars. Not only the brightest: Arcturus, twenty-five times bigger than the sun; Vega, Capella; but a champagne fizz of others that fill the sky.

I walk, stumbling into the dunes, craning my neck to look up, losing my way and direction. I give up and sling down my backpack, getting out my bivvy and sleeping bag.

By the time I lie down, the sky has solidified and set. The stars reach from hill to hill. With not even a hint of light pollution, there is no dead zone. No glowing star-less space that reaches from the horizon. Above me, the Milky Way rips the sky in two. A smudge. A chef-ish smear, as if the stars have been spread with the back of a spoon.

It is the clearest view of the Milky Way I have ever seen. It's hypnotising. Staring into this froth of stars and gas blooms is like looking into the depths of some kind of crystal where the flaws and cuts give the impression of multiple depths, of dizzying trenches, mountain ranges and yawning chasms.

I look through my binoculars, trying not to be overwhelmed by the scale of the starscape. There is an absurdity to it. An existential absurdity which, as philosopher Albert Camus said, comes from trying to seek meaning and purpose in a world that is irrational and meaningless. The old dictum goes that it is only the individual who can give both their life and their world meaning. But there is something immensely freeing about being as 'meaningless' as the stars.

I pull my sleeping bag up around my chin. The temperature has plunged tonight. The stars burn with cold. Their light wheyish, hard dots. Somewhere to the north, the motorway roar of the sea is loud, alongside the rumbling lows of cows. From the machair in front of me I can see a gathering of dark shapes.

Slightly nervous after previous cattle encounters, when I have woken up with them too close for comfort, I rummage for a torch, flicking it on to send a wobbling beam over grass already lightly crystallised with a sugar of frost. The hills, it seems, have eyes: tapetum lucidum that glint an ominous shade of teal.

The glowing eyes of livestock have unsettled hardier

souls than me. A friend of mine, a former Para and member of the Special Forces, used to train regularly in the Brecon Beacons. He told me how, during one sleepless twenty-four-hour 'tab', which had done for three of his toenails, he had got lost. After taking army painkillers that served only to heighten his sleep-deprived confusion, his torch beam had reflected back off hundreds of eyes watching him. In a panic, he threw his weapon at them, told them to take him, kill him; he was done.

He spent the next hour searching for his gun in a field of confused-looking sheep.

I turn the torch off and nestle back down in my sleeping bag in the hope they'll leave me be.

I close my eyes. Just resting them, as my grandad would have said. Just resting.

I wake with a jerk. A real jerk. Something is yanking at my bivvy bag. I shout instinctively and thrash my legs. My fugged brain tries to work out what to do.

Black bear, make noise, grizzly bear, stay calm.

I find my torch again and shine it towards my feet. The eyes of a Hebridean cow, made murderous by the glow from its retinas, stare back.

'Gnaargh,' I say.

The cow pauses and snorts.

'Piss off. Get. Go on.'

I slap the top of the bivvy bag. It seems to do the trick. The cow ambles off slowly, flashing me a shit-matted rump.

I check my gear. The bag is slobbered and a large muddy hoof print has been left between where my feet were resting. I pack and decide to move up the coast, heading for a beach where the cattle are less likely to roam.

I walk towards the Plough, the moon rising north through Taurus. Orion still crouched under the horizon, marching towards the edge of the southern hemisphere. My shadow is the darkest thing in a landscape dripping with moonlight.

I'm surprised by the amount of information I've soaked up about the stars, how much, with even my rookie experience and big gaps in knowledge, I can read them. While the Plough is the easiest way to find Polaris – the North Star – the pointers forever tethered to it during the asterism's anti-clockwise spin, there are other ways.

The Northern Cross at the heart of Cygnus also points to the Lode Star. Tristan Gooley, in his book *The Walker's Guide to Outdoor Clues & Signs*, suggests thinking of the cross as the Crucifix, with Jesus's right hand pointing to the Pole Star. Auriga, the Charioteer (which to my eyes looks more like a wonky barn), also can help find the Polaris. By following the lean of its collapsing, obtuse side, you can find the star that sits directly above the earth's axis.

Even when the North Star is obscured, it's still possible to work out direction, although it can take more time. While the points at which the moon, the planets and the sun rise change over days, weeks and months, the place on the horizon where stars rise remains constant. Of course, the stars move (or appear to with earth's spin) and the time they rise changes but their path, their trajectory, is always the same.

Part of me wants to capture the view of the stars above me on film, to be able to share it and look back at it again. My phone is next to useless, the photo showing nothing but a coalsack blackness. Even if I did have the gear to do it, the sky of pixels would bear little resemblance to the night of the naked eye. The long exposure, capable of capturing so much more light than the human retina, shows the sky in colour. The heat of stars picked out in clear reds and whites, the dust clouds, black against a mauve sky bubbled in light. It is interesting but unreal. I worry too that if a picture is the only way you've seen the Milky Way, the real thing would be a disappointment. It is sky porn.

The Plough is tilting by the time I'm sitting on the beach, digging deeper into the black sky. Dragging over rock and sea to spit up light for the few seabirds that for some reason still haven't settled. With the moon hidden behind bluff and rock, the view of the stars is fantastic.

I feel utterly at peace, a strange glassy sensation. I wish on a shooting star that flares and dies like a matchhead. My hands are cold. My face numb. My nose a thermostat that smells and feels the hard burn of frost. I think it might be my first of the year. I can see my bag is sparkling. Maybe I am too.

I wake at dawn, dusted with sand and cold to the bone. I stretch and creak before setting off back to the car across sand frozen into hard ruts. My footprints have been washed away on the beach but back on the machair they are there still, a trace of the night that lingers in the rough grass.

I walk back from the hotel with a bottle of wine as the sun sets. The western horizon is lit with litmus shades, growing from bright whites to deep alkaline blue. To the east the dark is already creeping, like damp up a wall.

The children have spent the day playing in the stream that feeds down into the loch. After the first two days when they kicked about the flat and squabbled, asking, 'Exactly why is this a holiday?' they've discovered the creativity and freedom that sometimes only boredom brings.

They explore and roam wherever they want, building dams, skimming stones, scrambling over rocks and shouting to seals, which pop their heads out of the water to inspect this new curious noise source. They are out for three or four hours at a time. Coming back tired, hungry and often wet; dragging kelp whips and scallop shells, their pockets full of crab claws and winkles.

They've also, completely unbidden, started writing. I can hardly believe it. They make a book whose cover glitters with stars and contains stories of adventurers, smugglers, pirates and shipwrecks – of which Coll has a rich history. Most famously the *Nevada*, the island's own *Whisky Galore!*, sunk in fog during 1942. The locals scooped up booze, hair cream and fags, hiding loot in the alcoves of their cottages and wallpapering over them until the authorities gave up the hunt.

We had planned on a quiet night in but with the gift of another clear sky, I'm itching to get out. Using the promise of a late night and a Thermos of hot chocolate as leverage, I persuade the kids and Jen to join me, all of us trooping to the car in layers of jumpers, coats, hats and gloves.

Not far from Arnabost, I pull in by a metal gate that carries a sign for the beach. On the other side the track is clear and we walk along a trail of pale stone that leads past a darkened farmhouse and into the machair.

The path fades but I insist we keep going. The kids bouncing along with us behind. Further in, surrounded by hillocks of the grass, I lose the trail again. If I was on my own, I'd not be worried, but Jen is understandably getting snippy. She said she thought I'd been here before and is quietly incredulous that for all my surface confidence, I don't know where the hell we are going.

She tells Seth, who is still trying to race off ahead, to stay close and shoots me a look as we tiptoe around a pond brimful of cold, deep, darkness.

I suggest we stop where we are, but the kids are keen to keep moving. I'd said beach and beach they want. I think they are also relishing the tension: revelling in the fact that it's Dad getting told off and not them.

I try to shush them so I can hear the direction of the sea, its roar. We squelch up and down the black sponge of machair. Eventually a path emerges and we follow it to a dune edge that drops steeply to a white beach whose pools glimmer with starlight.

We stop. Open the flask of hot chocolate and perch in the dunes.

We talk in a hushed whisper as if the stars would be scared away. But they are bold and bright again tonight. I point out constellations to the children but I don't think they really care. They're in it for the bigger picture, the sheer mass, the thousands of suns whose light is older than anything they will ever know.

It is the first time too that they have seen the Milky Way. They gasp at its spray of light, and wrestle with the idea of how they can see the galaxy they are in. We try describing it together. Milk spray. Frost. Mould. Sea foam. Salt stains. Seth hits on the same simile as I had the night before: a topsy-turvy view from a plane, the bright lights not towns and roads, but stars millions of miles, light years apart.

Then the shooting stars begin. I hadn't told the children I was hoping to see Orionids as I didn't want them to be disappointed, but now they whoop and holler at every flaring, dusty streak. Red lights. A tinge of gassy green. We fall silent between each one and I will the kids to stay interested. In my head I tell them, hold your nerve and let the night take you.

I feel so happy that everyone is here and enjoying themselves. I squeeze Jen's hand and whisper, 'Thank you.' Over-excited, I try to get everyone to lie down, to see the night. To feel it.

'It's as if the stars are pulling you.'

They look down at me, the stars' spell broken, and answer in incredulous unison. No, Dad, it's freezing. And there's too much goose poo.

Their fidgets grow with the cold and the dwindling hot chocolate. We retrace our steps and drive back slowly, the children's chatter excited and bubbling. Everyone is glowing and luminous, retinas night-soaked and star-burned.

Back at the apartment the kids scramble out of the car first and are instantly laughing. Eliza points at the sky and the Milky Way that shimmers across the sky and sea.

'Oh, Dad, we could have just stayed here.'

I can't sleep. It's the first night here that I've woken before the morning light pours through the window. I toss and turn and keep checking the clock. The hours crawl, from night's quietest quarter to nearly touching dawn.

I get up so I don't disturb Jen and set the fire. There's still heat pulsing from last night's embers and I add new

183

pieces of coal, turning them to help them catch. Outside the sky is still dark, the distinction between sea and sky only the merest of dark lines.

I pull on my boots and heaviest coat and go outside. The cloud has moved in and the wind has returned. The air, blown over water and kelp, smells clean and deliciously cold. I can feel it move in me. Down my throat and into my lungs.

Over at the new pier, the gate and fences clang with the wind. Orion stands with a club raised over the jaw of a fin whale set into the hill. These bones are a replica, the originals safe in the National Museum of Scotland. The whale was washed up on Feal beach, where I slept two nights ago, and when the crown claimed it, two locals severed the jaw with a chainsaw, hiding it for weeks in a sand dune. It was returned, under the cover of darkness, only when the police (travelling over from the mainland) threatened prosecution.

Real or not, the bones are a good monument. A symbol of defiance against the elements and the encroaching of modernity. An upended white V-sign against night's retreat. The first sight for new visitors leaving the ferry.

Soon they will be the last view I have of the island as I head back south, away from the dark.

I walk onto the pier, nearly castrating myself on a night-shaded bollard set at perfect bollock-scraping height, and climb over the barrier that's put in place when the ferry isn't in. I walk cautiously. I sometimes have a fear of walking out to sea. An aesthetic jarring, as if the brain can't quite believe it's safe. I've even felt it among the electric lights of Brighton's pier, where I walk in the centre of the fenced boardwalk to avoid that sudden pang of vertigo.

Here in the dark, with the noise of water and wind, the fear grows. I stand as close to the edge as I dare. The night may be ebbing but still it wraps around me. I hold onto the rail, feeling its solidity, as if I might be carried off by the sea, by the dark.

Standing there, fingers numb on the railings, I think of all the nights I've walked in. The snow, the cloud, the clear skies, moonlight and murk, starfall and darkrise. Each night, whether it contained happiness, wonder, fear or frustration, has been unique; each experience has shown me darkness in a different light.

My friend Isabel told me how when she was up at all hours with her young son, she used to console herself with the thought that she was living twice as long. I know what she means. Being open to the night has shown me a different world to the one I was used to. To be open to the night, to welcome it, embrace it, rather than shut it out, does bring with it an extra richness. To walk at night has been a night twice lived.

The experiences have been eye-opening in other ways; they have made me realise how much night and our expectations of it have changed. The darkness, and with it the subtle natural light of the moon and stars, the dizzying shifts of twilight, are all being lost to the ever-expanding creep of artificial light. The natural night has shrunk back, slunk into the shadows to hide in reserves and far-flung locations, both in the UK and across the world. Of course Dark Sky Reserves and Discovery Sites are vital. But they should only be starting points.

Many nature reserves were founded in response to emergencies – saving ancient trees from bulldozers, fenland valleys from boreholes and drainage. But there is now an acknowledgement that for wildlife to survive, to thrive, it must be allowed to spread from these biodiverse points through networks of wildness: hedgerows, field margins, verges, parks, gardens, villages, towns and cities. The same is true of night. These special places – where darkness and natural night hold on – are capable of sparking inspiration; showing people in even urban locations that night is wondrous, ever-changing, yet continuous. They allow people to connect with the night, to share the ancient lights that have illuminated the acts and thoughts of humans throughout their existence. They allow us to question our place in the universe, but also the use of artificial lights in our lives.

By tuning in, there is a greater chance of us also turning off, to let night grow across our island. Perhaps even in towns and cities there will be a recognition that the spread and saturation of artificial light, which damages both wildlife and us, is as problematic as the plastic particles that hang suspended in our rivers and seas – but so much easier to solve. By lighting our world sparingly, carefully, perhaps we could learn to appreciate the beauty of a natural night again.

I turn around and begin walking back along the pier. I would love to stay on Coll for longer; to fall into its dusky embrace, to be washed, soothed and confronted by the dark. To cling to the soft lights of night.

Acknowledgements

This book would have been impossible without the generosity, knowledge, insight and support of a number of people. Some were friends and loved ones, others academics and pint-sippers who probably had far better things to be getting on with.

First, I would like to thank my urban Sherpa Shaun Norris for braving storm-lash and city lights with me. Thanks also to Sam Norris for letting me borrow him so close to the birth of little Logan. I am also indebted to Olly Cranford for introducing me to 'deer ears' and joining me on another, unrecorded, nocturnal stomp. A hat-tip too for Sean Torfinn, who provided some useful and much-needed tips about not dying.

I am immensely grateful too for the input of a number of brilliant academics, experts and aficionados who answered my sometimes rambling questions with eloquence and enthusiasm. So, thank you Travis Longcore, Jon Bennie, Bob Mizon, Emma Marrington, Dan Hillier and Stuart Peirson. I would also like to thank David and the whole team at the Scottish Dark Sky Observatory in Galloway.

Thank you also to the community of Coll, especially Paula, Kip and the drinkers at the Coll Hotel who were helpful and welcoming in equal measure.

Thanks too must go to the team at Suffolk Wildlife Trust's Lackford Lakes, who just about put up with me writing in their office. Thumbs up in particular to Will Cranstoun, Joe Bell-Tye, Mike Andrews, Hawk Honey, Sophie Mayes, James Robinson and Paul Holness.

I would also like to give an especially big gilt-edged thank you to my dear friend Isabel Vogel, whose patient and insightful reading of early drafts of the book helped me to make it what it is. I owe her, both for my sanity and for 'palimpsest' – which, appropriately enough, was written over.

A huge thank you must also go to Jennie Condell, Pippa Crane and Sarah Rigby, the amazingly wonderful team at Elliott & Thompson. Their continued faith in

ACKNOWLEDGEMENTS

me, patience, tireless work and vision were crucial to making this book.

Thanks also to my friends and family whose support never waned, although their tendency to ask 'How's the book then?' thankfully did.

I would also like to remember my two wonderful grandparents, Jim and Tommy, who passed away during the writing of this book.

Finally, I would like to say thank you to Jen, Seth and Eliza, my moon, my stars, my everything. Their endless support and understanding has been indescribable. I love you all dearly and I promise we will go back to Coll soon.

Bibliography

Ackroyd, Peter, *The English Ghost: Spectres Through Time* (London: Vintage, 2011)

Adams, Richard, *Watership Down* (London: Puffin, 1973)

Beaumont, Matthew, *Nightwalking: A Nocturnal History of London* (London: Verso Books, 2013)

Belleville, Geneviève; Foldes-Busque, Guillaume; Dixon, Mélanie; Marquis-Pelletier, Évelyne; Barbeau, Sarah; Poitras, Julien; Chauny, Jean-Marc; Diodati, Jean G.; Fleet, Richard; Marchand, André, 'Impact of Seasonal and Lunar Cycles on Psychological Symptoms in the ED: An Empirical Investigation of Widely Spread Beliefs', *General Hospital Psychiatry*, vol. 35, no. 2, March–April 2013

Ben-Ari, Eyal, 'What Happens at Night, Stays at Night', *New Scientist*, 27 November 2013

Bogard, Paul, *The End of Night: Searching for Natural Darkness in an Age of Artificial Light* (London: Fourth Estate, 2014)

Boyle, Rebecca, 'Bright Skies at Night: The Riddle of the Nocturnal Sun', *New Scientist*, 19 December 2017

Brox, Jane, *Brilliant: The Evolution of Artificial Light* (London: Souvenir Press Ltd, 2012)

Burke, Edmund, *A Philosophical Enquiry into the Sublime and Beautiful* (London: Penguin Classics, 1998)

Capern, Edward, *Wayside Warbles* (London: Sampson Low, Son and Marston, 1865)

Castro, José J.; Pozo, Antonio M.; Rubiño, Manuel; Anera, Rosario G.; Jiménez del Barco, Luis, 'Retinal-Image Quality and Night-Vision Performance after Alcohol Consumption', *Journal of Ophthalmology*, vol. 24, 2014

Conan Doyle, Arthur, *The Hound of the Baskervilles* (London: Penguin Classics, 2007)

Da Silva, Arnaud; Valcu, Mihai; Kempenaers, Bart, 'Artificial night lighting causes birds to sing earlier', Max Planck Institute for Ornithology, 17 March 2015, https://www.mpg.de/9043097/light-pollution-songbirds

Dickens, Charles, *Night Walks* (London: Penguin Great Ideas, 2010)

Dunn, Nick, *Dark Matters: A Manifesto for the Nocturnal City* (Alresford, Hants: Zero Books, 2016)

Ekirch, A. Roger, *At Day's Close: A History of Nighttime* (London: W&N, new ed. 2006)

Falchi, Fabio; Cinzano, Pierantonio; Duriscoe, Dan; Kyba, Christopher C. M.; Elvidge, Christopher D.; Baugh, Kimberly; Portnov, Boris A.; Rybnikova, Nataliya A.; Furgoni, Riccardo, 'The New World Atlas of Artificial Night Sky Brightness', *Science Advances*, vol. 2, no. 6, June 2016

Gooley, Tristan, *The Walker's Guide to Outdoor Clues and Signs* (London: Sceptre, 2015)

'The Great British Bedtime Report', The Sleep Council, https://www.sleepcouncil.org.uk/wp-content/uploads/2013/02/The-Great-British-Bedtime-Report.pdf

Hamzelou, Jessica, 'The Night: Full Moon Mayhem Is for Real', *New Scientist*, 27 November 2013

'How Much Sleep Do We Need?', The Sleep Council, https://sleepcouncil.org.uk/how-much-sleep-do-we-need/

Hudston, Sara, 'Country Diary: A Bird Associated with Lost Souls and Otherworldly Forces', *Guardian*, 3 August 2018

Khazan, Olga, 'Thomas Edison and the Cult of Sleep Deprivation', *The Atlantic*, 14 May 2014

Koslofsky, Craig, *Evening's Empire: A History of the Night in Early Modern Europe* (Cambridge: Cambridge University Press, 2011)

Kyba, Christopher C. M.; Kuester, Theres; Sánchez de Miguel, Alejandro; Baugh, Kimberly; Jechow, Andreas; Hölker, Franz; Bennie, Jonathan; Elvidge, Christopher D.; Gaston, Kevin J.; Guanter, Luis, 'Artificially Lit Surface of Earth at Night Increasing in Radiance and Extent', *Science Advances*, vol. 3, no. 11, November 2017

Lawton, Graham, 'The Night: When Darkness Falls, Fear Rises', *New Scientist*, 27 November 2013

Leger, Damien, 'The Cost of Sleep-Related Accidents: A Report for the National Commission on Sleep Disorders Research', American Sleep Disorders Association and Sleep Research Society, *Sleep*, vol. 17, no. 1, 1994

Locke, John, *An Essay Concerning Human Understanding* (London: Penguin Classics, revised ed. 1998)

Loss, Scott; Will, Tom; Loss, Sara; Marra, Peter, 'Bird–Building Collisions in the United States: Estimates of Annual Mortality and Species Vulnerability', *The Condor*, 2014

McLaren, James D.; Buler, Jeff; Schreckengost, Tim; Smolinsky, Jaclyn; Boone, Matthew; van Loon, E.; Dawson, Deanna; Walters, Eric, 'Artificial Light at Night Confounds Broad-Scale Habitat Use by Migrating Birds', *Ecology Letters*, 2018

Mustard, Cameron A.; Chambers, Andrea; McLeod, Christopher; Bielecky, Amber; Smith, Peter M., 'Work Injury Risk by Time of Day in Two Population-Based Data Sources', *Occupational & Environmental Medicine*, vol. 70, no. 1, 2013

'Number of People Working Night Shifts Up by More Than 150,000 in 5 Years', Trades Union Congress, 27 October 2018, https://www.tuc.org.uk/news/number-peopl e-working-night-shifts-more-150000-5-years

O'Callaghan, Tiffany, 'The Night: Why They Call It the Graveyard Shift', *New Scientist*, 27 November 2013

Rich, Catherine and Longcore, Travis (eds), *Ecological Consequences of Artificial Night Lighting* (Washington, DC: Island Press, 2013)

Steinbach, Rebecca; Perkins, Chloe; Tompson, Lisa; Johnson, Shane; Armstrong, Ben; Green, Judith; Grundy, Chris; Wilkinson, Paul; Edwards, Phil, 'The Effect of Reduced Street Lighting on Road Casualties and Crime in England and Wales: Controlled Interrupted Time Series Analysis', *Journal of Epidemiology and Community Health*, vol. 69, 2015

Stroud, Richard, *The Book of the Moon* (London: Doubleday, 2009)

Thoreau, Henry David, *Night and Moonlight* (CreateSpace Independent Publishing Platform, 2015)

Yi-Fu Tuan, 'The City: Its Distance from Nature', *Geographical Review*, vol. 68, no. 1, January 1978

White, Jonathan, *Tides: The Science and Spirit of the Ocean* (San Antonio, TX: Trinity University Press, 2017)

Yates, Chris, *Nightwalk: A Journey to the Heart of Nature* (London: William Collins, 2014)

Endnotes

1. Hamzelou, Jessica, 'The Night: Full Moon Mayhem Is for Real', *New Scientist*, 27 November 2013.
2. Geneviève Belleville et al., 'Impact of Seasonal and Lunar Cycles on Psychological Symptoms in the ED: An Empirical Investigation of Widely Spread Beliefs', *General Hospital Psychiatry*, vol. 35, no. 2, October 2012.
3. Act IV, Scene I.
4. A. Roger Ekirch, *At Day's Close: A History of Nighttime* (London: W&N, new ed. 2006).
5. José J. Castro et al., 'Retinal-Image Quality and Night-Vision Performance after Alcohol Consumption', *Journal of Ophthalmology*, vol. 24, 2014.
6. Ekirch, *At Day's Close*.
7. Ibid.
8. Matthew Beaumont, *Nightwalking: A Nocturnal History of London* (London: Verso Books, 2013).
9. Ekirch, *At Day's Close*, p. 325.
10. Yi-Fu Tuan, 'The City: Its Distance from Nature', *Geographical Review*, vol. 68, no. 1, January 1978.
11. Ibid.
12. https://www.sleepcouncil.org.uk/wp-content/uploads/2013/02/The-Great-British-Bedtime-Report.pdf
13. https://sleepcouncil.org.uk/how-much-sleep-do-we-need/

14. Cameron A. Mustard et al., 'Work Injury Risk by Time of Day in Two Population-Based Data Sources', *Occupational & Environmental Medicine*, vol. 70, no. 1, 2012.

15. The World Health Organisation classified night-shift work as a probable carcinogen in 2007.

16. Christopher C. M. Kyba et al., 'Artificially Lit Surface of Earth at Night Increasing in Radiance and Extent', *Science Advances*, vol. 3, no. 11, November 2017.

17. Scott Loss et al., 'Bird–Building Collisions in the United States: Estimates of Annual Mortality and Species Vulnerability', *The Condor*, 2014.

18. James D. McLaren et al, 'Artificial Light at Night Confounds Broad-Scale Habitat Use by Migrating Birds', *Ecology Letters*, 2018.

19. Rebecca Steinbach et al., 'The Effect of Reduced Street Lighting on Road Casualties and Crime in England and Wales: Controlled Interrupted Time Series Analysis', *Journal of Epidemiology and Community Health*, vol. 69, 2015.

20. Catherine Rich and Travis Longcore (eds), *Ecological Consequences of Artificial Night Lighting* (Washington, DC: Island Press, 2013), p. 32.

21. Richard Adams, *Watership Down* (London: Puffin, 1973), p. 60.

Index

INDEX

INDEX

INDEX

INDEX